The European Texans

TEXANS ALL

A Series from
the Institute of Texan Cultures
Sara R. Massey, General Editor

The European Texans

Allan O. Kownslar

TEXAS A&M UNIVERSITY PRESS · COLLEGE STATION

The Ellwood Foundation, Houston, Texas, provided funding
support for the research and writing of this book.

The paper used in this book
meets the minimum requirements
of the American National Standard for Permanence
of Paper for Printed Library Materials, z39.48-1984.
Binding materials have been chosen for durability.

∞

Illustrations on the title page and chapter heads are
details from the map by Jack Jackson found on page 2.

LIBRARY OF CONGRESS CATALOGING-IN-PUBLICATION DATA

Kownslar, Allan O.

    The European Texans / Allan O. Kownslar.—1st ed.

      p. cm.—(Texans all)

    Includes bibliographical references and index.

    ISBN 1-58544-351-4 (alk. paper)—

    ISBN 1-58544-352-2 (pbk. : alk. paper)

    1. European Americans—Texas—History. 2. European Americans—
Texas—Social life and customs. 3. Immigrants—Texas—History. 4. Texas—
Ethnic relations. 5. Texas—Emigration and immigration—History. 6. Europe—
Emigration and immigration—History. I. University of Texas Institute of Texan
Cultures at San Antonio. II. Title. III. Series.

F395.E95K68   2004   •

976.4'00409—dc22   2003016359

Contents

Illustrations

▼▼▼

▼▼▼

Foreword

The Institute of Texan Cultures opened in 1968 with exhibits depicting the cultural groups that had settled early Texas. The displays resulted from a massive research effort by many young scholars into the history and culture of Texas. This research served as the basis for writing what became known as "the ethnic pamphlet series." The series included pamphlets devoted to such titles as the Swiss Texans, the Norwegian Texans, the Native American Texans, the Mexican Texans, the Greek Texans, the Spanish Texans, the African American Texans, the Chinese Texans, and many more. Some years later several books about additional cultural groups were produced, including the Japanese Texans, the Irish Texans, the Polish Texans, and numerous others.

Years later, as staff reviewed the early pamphlets, they realized that although the material remained accurate, it was time for a major revision with a fresh look. Thus emerged the Texans All book set. Organized by cultural groups, each volume briefly summarizes aspects of the social and cultural contributions made by several groups who immigrated to Texas. The book set includes the five distinct cultural groups that already existed in Texas prior to its statehood or who came to Texas in the early twentieth century: *The Indian Texans, The Mexican Texans, The European Texans, The African Texans,* and *The Asian Texans.*

The author of each book used an organizational pattern dictated by the content. *The European Texans* is organized by the nation-states within the major geographic regions of Europe. Given the changing map of Europe during the past two centuries, no categories really seemed to fit. So the author has chosen a simple north, south, east, west system used by geographers in mapping the regions of Europe. Additionally, the content does not follow the traditional history of battles and events in Texas but rather addresses the culture and the people as they formed early communities in Texas.

The authors also searched for primary sources to incorporate within the text, and sidebars are occasionally utilized to provide brief biographical or topical sketches. As the manuscripts neared completion, maps were commissioned to illustrate the initial settlement areas of the various cultural groups in Texas.

The experiences of a person or family that settled in Texas provide a personalized introduction to several of the cultural groups in *The European Texans*. Although some famous Texans are discussed, most of the people presented are ordinary people who struggled to build a home and make a living in Texas. The majority of the over three hundred photographs used in the book set are from the Institute of Texan Cultures Research Library's extensive photograph collection of over three million images relating to the people and cultures of Texas.

Explorers from the various European cultural regions began arriving in the 1500s with sporadic settlement in the 1600s and 1700s. However, extensive settlement in Texas did not get under way until the mid-1800s. For several groups, an individual or a family would arrive and then write letters home. The letters told about the wonderful opportunities in Texas, prompting more settlers to head for Texas. Each group of people that came brought aspects of their culture with them whether it was their unique language, an old family recipe for spaghetti sauce, or folktales of their homeland. It is from the rich cultural diversity of Europe that Texas grew. Though history is often buried in death—from wars, disease, violence, and natural disasters—it is the celebration of life in the customs and rituals of a diverse people that is the focus here.

While some content from the ethnic pamphlet series is included, additional information has been incorporated. *The European Texans* does not attempt to include people from all the European countries who settled in Texas or the people arriving from the "United States" called Anglos, who were often the children of first- or second-generation European immigrants. These European Americans from the United States came to represent the majority population in Texas but are not presented here. Additionally, the many immigrants to Mexico and Texas from Spain, a European country, are not included here but rather are detailed in *The Mexican Texans* since their culture and history fits more appropriately within that context.

While significant immigration to Texas from the various European nations continued into the twentieth century, this book introduces us to the early groups that arrived and started the numerous towns and communities of Texas up to about 1910. As generations passed and marriages occurred, many immigrants lost their "old-world" identities, but many of their delightful stories, recipes, institutions, and organizations they brought remain.

The number of colonists from each nation and their relative importance in Texas changed over time. Problems back home significantly influenced when large numbers of colonists might seek new opportunities. Not all colonists of early Texas found wealth and happiness. The problems and hardships as well as prejudice and discrimination encountered by some groups were numerous, and frequently folks returned home. But for those that stayed, a state unlike others emerged. Texas became home, and all left their imprint as they became Texan.

Sara R. Massey

Acknowledgments

The author wishes to recognize the research and writing of the early researchers at the Institute of Texan Cultures. The legacy of their fine work made the compilation of this volume on eighteen cultural groups of European Texans possible.

All recipes included are from *The Melting Pot: Ethnic Cuisine in Texas,* published by the Institute of Texan Cultures, 1997, unless otherwise noted.

The European Texans

EUROPEAN TEXANS

Settlement to 1900

European settlement areas in Texas. Map by Jack Jackson

Introduction

Texas has been a meeting place of people and cultures from throughout the world. From prehistory into the 1600s the native people, who came to be called Indians, roamed the land that eventually became Texas. Not until the early 1500s did the first people from Europe arrive—the Spanish. Friars, soldiers, colonists, and native people came north from New Spain to settle the northern frontier that would become Texas. In the late 1700s and 1800s settlers came from various regions of the United States, many bringing with them their African slaves and the predominant English culture of the country. During the early 1800s many single men from various European nations came to Texas on the western frontier. Following the close of the Napoleonic Wars in 1815, approximately 143,000 immigrants came to the United States between 1821 and 1830. Some of them made port in New Orleans and went on to Texas.

Between 1831 and 1869 many European immigrants came to America, primarily from Ireland and Germany. This period is frequently referred to as "the first wave" of immigration. Immigration slowed during the Civil War, but following its conclusion and as the result of the emergence of reliable oceanic transportation, some six million Europeans arrived in the United States from 1861 to 1890, a period referred to as "the great migration."[1] Between 1842 and 1878 the Adelsverein, an immigrant organization composed of German nobility, induced about sixty thousand immigrants to settle in Texas. By the early 1900s the Europeans in Texas and their descendants numbered in the thousands.

Greek immigrants on board a ship coming to America. Institute of Texan Cultures no. 68-2721

The European Texans presents people from eighteen European cultural groups who immigrated to Texas between the early 1800s and 1910. The cultural groups were selected for the variety of life they have brought to Texas and are organized by the general geographical regions of Europe. The major nations of western Europe provided us with people of French, English, Scottish, Irish, Dutch, Belgian, and Swiss heritage. From northern Europe came the Danes, Norwegians, and Swedes while immigrants from eastern Europe included Germans, Wends (from Prussia), Poles, Czechs, and Hungarians. The Italians from Italy and Sicily, the Greeks, and the Serbs/Slavs/Croatians who left the portion of the Austrian-Hungarian Empire that now comprises Yugoslavia are included from the southern European region. People thus came to Texas from virtually all regions of Europe.

While early census data are difficult to obtain and the manner of categorizing information varies from census to census, tables 1–4 present the number of foreign-born among the cultural groups who resided in Texas during the years 1870, 1890, 1900, and 1910.

▼▼▼

TABLE 1. FOREIGN BORN FROM WESTERN EUROPE

	1870	1890	1900	1910
French	2,232	2,730	2,025	1,821
English	2,090	9,443	8,213	8,498
Scots	620	2,172	1,952	2,038
Irish	4,144	8,201	6,173	5,357
Dutch	54	130	262	424
Belgians	73	216	244	328
Swiss	599	1,711	1,709	1,773

Sources for tables 1–4: A Compendium of the Ninth Census 1870 (U.S. Government Printing Office, 1872), 435–37, 393; *Compendium of the Tenth Census of 1880* (U.S. Government Printing Office, 1883), 531–34; *Compendium of the Eleventh Census of 1890* (U.S. Government Printing Office, 1894), 600–603, 686–89; *Abstract of the Twelfth Census of 1900* (U.S. Government Printing Office, 1902), 56–63; *Abstract of the Thirteenth Census of 1910* (U.S. Government Printing Office, 1913), 206–207.

TABLE 2. FOREIGN BORN FROM NORTHERN EUROPE

	1870	1890	1900	1910
Danes	159	649	1,089	1,289
Norwegians	403	1,313	1,359	1,785
Swedes	364	2,896	4,388	4,706

TABLE 3. FOREIGN BORN FROM EASTERN EUROPE

	1870	1890	1900	1910
Germans	23,985	48,843	48,295	44,929
Wends	710 (est.)	500 (est.)	n.d.[a]	n.d.
Poles	448	1,591	3,348	n.d.
Czechs (Bohemia only)	781	3,215	9,204	n.d.
Hungarians	46	228	593	926

[a]The abbreviation "n.d." denotes that the census summary did not include a category that year for that particular ethnic group.

TABLE 4. FOREIGN BORN FROM SOUTHERN EUROPE

	1870	1890	1900	1910
Italians	186	2,107	3,952	7,190
Greeks	38	145	169	756
Serbs/Slavs/Croatians	12 (est.)	80 (est.)	120 (est.)	n.d.

In Rio Hondo, Texas, the land company had a hotel for immigrants to stay upon their arrival, ca. 1910. Institute of Texan Cultures no. 72-2049

The 1880 federal census summaries included data for only three of the groups addressed in this volume: Irish, 6,955; Scots, 1,667; and French, 2,668; and combined the total for the Norwegians and the Swedes, 2,178. Population totals for the Wends and the Serbs/Slavs/Croatians can only be estimates since during the 1800s these people were part of populations governed by distinct countries such as Prussia, Austria, and Serbia, and boundaries changed frequently based on local events. The same is true for census summary data about the Poles and Czechs in 1910. Most Poles were then under Russian rule and Czechs under Austrian domination. The children

▼▼▼

or spouses born in the United States or spouses of another ethnic origin are not included in the numbers.

The largest number of early immigrants came primarily from western and eastern European countries, with the majority coming from Ireland and Germany. The Germans, who began arriving in the 1840s, were the largest European immigrant group. Immigration following the Civil War shifted to include those from northern and southern Europe, but Germans continued to arrive in Texas in large numbers. Large numbers of Jewish people also immigrated to Texas, but they came from many different countries throughout Europe, and are not incorporated here as a distinct group from any one nation.

The journey to Texas typically began at one of many European ports. The Germans and the Czechs usually left through the North German ports of Bremen or Hamburg. Swedes departed through Goeborg and the Norwegians from Stavanger or Christiansand. The Irish immigrants went to Liverpool on England's west coast and transferred to ships sailing to America. The Belgians, Dutch, and some French sailed from L'Harve, and Naples was the primary exit port for Italians coming to America.

At the wharf in Galveston, immigrants walked the mile or so to the train depot where an amazing site greeted them. "Often a Russian, or a German from Hamburg, could be seen wearing a fur coat in July or August, or a Swiss peasant . . . in native attire with knee breeches and Alpine hat decorated with feathers. These were the days when females here wore anklets and showed nothing more than their insteps. To behold the peasant women of Germany and Switzerland with dresses up to their knees made everybody 'rubberneck.'"[2]

The first arrivals in the early 1800s were usually single men who were adventurers, soldiers, or men desperate for a new chance in life. By the 1830s some leader or well-known person of status, sometimes with family, would move to and settle in Texas. Then he would write glowing letters home to family or friends about the wonderful qualities of Texas. These letters often were printed in the local

▼▼▼

newspaper. This provided the encouragement, support, or stimulus for others to make the decision to immigrate. Why the diverse ethnic groups initially decided to come to Texas, when and where they first settled, how they made a living, as well as the amazing array of customs and foods they brought with them is addressed here through a brief overview of the early European settlers.

Europeans who came to Texas during the nineteenth and early twentieth centuries did so for a variety of reasons. Some wanted to escape required enlistment as soldiers in the numerous and devastating European wars. Others grew tired of discrimination against their way of life. Many were weary of living in poverty or frustrated in attempts to own their own land or prosper in their trade. Crop failures for small farmers forced many off their land. The tax burden in some countries along with social restrictions and political repression caused even more to leave their homelands. Some simply sought adventure and excitement. The mid-1800s in Europe also was a time plagued by agrarian crisis and political inequalities. For many the choice to leave home and seek their future elsewhere was the only option that offered hope. But whether coming in large or small numbers, each group brought cultural artifacts and values of their homeland to Texas.

Once in Texas, immigrants faced extreme and severe weather conditions such as drought or hurricanes, hostile Indians, disease, loneliness, initial lack of most basics and luxuries, homesickness, and the difficult adjustment to curious surroundings. Some immigrants like the Poles and Czechs faced prejudice as people made fun of their language or the way they dressed. Others were victims of Texas' Alien Land Law of April 12, 1892. This law prohibited the acquisition of land by aliens and required foreign nationals holding land in Texas to dispose of their property or to become United States citizens within ten years.[3] America during the 1890s was very xenophobic (fearful of foreigners), and in Texas, once part of the old Confederacy, the "Jim Crow" laws (racial segregation) and prejudices were rampant.

▼▼▼

To help overcome such problems, many people, with exceptions such as the English and the Scots, preferred to locate with others like themselves, settling with those from their homeland who spoke the same language and had similar customs. Even today in Texas many German, Czech, Pole, and Norwegian descendants reside in the communities started by their great-grandparents. Some found the problems too much to bear and returned to their homelands, but the majority of the hearty settlers stayed, survived, and became part of the heritage of Texas.

During the latter half of the twentieth century, a renewed interest in the diversity of cultural life in Texas occurred as various ethnic organizations and individuals began to delve into their family history to preserve some of their unique European culture. Much of that curiosity now can be fulfilled at the Texas Folklife Festival conducted annually by the University of Texas Institute of Texan Cultures at San Antonio as well as through its exhibits and publications.

The stories of the European Texans have combined to create a rich tradition in a place that is uniquely Texan.

CHAPTER 1
Western Europe

THE FRENCH TEXANS

1870: 2,232
1890: 2,730
1900: 2,025
1910: 1,821

Early Texas was originally Spanish territory as part of New Spain, but the French were very interested in the land west of their thriving port of New Orleans. Imagine pirates being some of the first settlers in Texas. That was the case for the French Laffite brothers, Pierre and his younger brother, Jean. Pierre and Jean were among the numerous pirates and smugglers along the Gulf Coast. Pierre, the real leader of the two, directed their illegal activities from Barataria Island, off the Louisiana coast. In 1814 they had to abandon the Barataria operation when United States authorities seized their stolen goods.

Jean Laffite hoped to get back in the good graces of the U.S. government, so during the War of 1812, he and his fellow pirates fought with Andrew Jackson's army when it defeated the British forces January 8, 1815, at the battle of New Orleans. Jean then presented his appeal before President James Madison to get back his confiscated property. Madison turned him down.

Over the years the Laffite brothers kept changing allegiances. First, they pledged to help the Spanish government, and then they

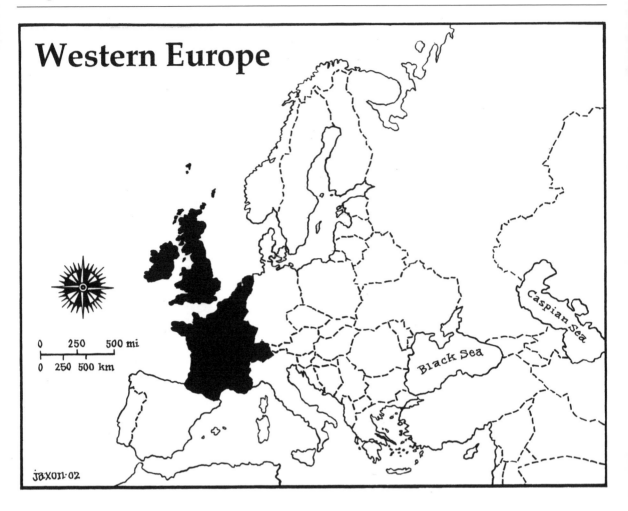

Western Europe

0   250   500 mi

0   250   500 km

Caspian Sea

Black Sea

jaxon·02

Western Europe. Map by Jack Jackson

switched to help the Mexicans who wanted to overthrow Spanish rule in Texas. This led them to Galveston Island in 1817 where they dislodged Louis Michel Aury, another French pirate, and began the community of Campeche.

Jean made Campeche his new base camp for looting and set up what he called a "Pirate Republic." He named his house—a red structure with cannons pointed out the second floor windows—Maison Rouge. All the while, the United States and Spain were unable to halt the piracies of Laffite and his men. Finally, though, the Laffite brothers raided one too many American ships. Afraid of what the new American president James Monroe might do, the Laffites in

▼▼▼

1820 decided to abandon their Galveston retreat. They sailed from Texas on their favorite vessel, *The Pride,* to Mugeres Island, off the coast of Yucatán. There they continued with their pirating until Jean died in 1825.

Fortunately, the French piracy elements in Texas were confined to such men as the Laffite brothers and Aury. Some Frenchmen, such as René Robert Cavelier, Sieur de La Salle, who had sailed from France in 1684, came to the area on more legitimate business. After missing the mouth of the Mississippi River and losing his ships (including one that returned to France), he tried unsuccessfully to establish a colony called Fort St. Louis on Garcitas Creek, three miles from Lavaca Bay along the coast of the Gulf of Mexico.

Stranded without supplies and threatened by the Karankawas, La Salle and some of his men began a long trek trying to reach French Canada. As they traveled north, La Salle was killed by one of his men. Some men on the trip managed to get to French Canada, and a few even made it back to France. Those who were forced to remain at the settlement were attacked by a band of Karankawas who killed all except five children who were taken captive. Members of a Spanish expedition searching for the French colony later ransomed the children from the tribe, and three of the children eventually made it back to France.

Another early French presence in Texas was Louis Juchereau de St. Denis who built a trading post at Natchitoches on the French side of the Red River. From Natchitoches, in 1714, he crossed into Spanish Texas and made his way to the Rio Grande on a trading expedition. However, further French involvement in Texas stalled when on the continent France and Spain went to war against one another. The Spanish in Texas then drove the French back into Louisiana. Only when peace resumed between France and Spain did a few Frenchmen from Louisiana again initiate trade among the Indian tribes in East Texas.

At Champ d'Asile, a military camp on the Trinity River near present-day Liberty between Houston and Beaumont, French soldiers made an attempt to gain a foothold in Spanish East Texas.

This settlement effort involved four hundred veterans from the Napoleonic Wars who arrived in 1818. They were followers of the defeated dictator Napoleon and wanted to rescue him from his exile on the island of St. Helena and make him emperor of Mexico. They failed not only in their attempt to rescue Napoleon but also in their Texas settlement.

The impractical French soldiers at Champ d'Asile, more accustomed to soldiering than farming, held military drills rather than spend time raising needed food crops. When threatened by the Spanish, who still claimed the area, and the failure of their few crops, most of the settlers fled after a mere six months to Galveston Island. Laffite first thought to betray the French to the Spaniards, but eventually he provided some of the Frenchmen from Champ d'Asile with a captured Spanish vessel to return to France. A few remaining Frenchmen walked overland to New Orleans.

Other French settled in Texas after the Laffites left Galveston. Among them were those who supported the Texas Revolution against Mexico. Michel Menard, a French Canadian, was a signer of the Texas Declaration of Independence of 1836. Menard later became a cotton salesman in Galveston and brought the first French Roman Catholic priests to Texas. Peter Menard, Michel's brother, also fought in the Texas Revolution. He later became Galveston's first postmaster. Dr. Nicholas Labadie, another French Canadian, served with Sam Houston's army during the Texas Revolution. He provided needed medical help to the soldiers. He later opened the first drugstore in Galveston, owned a line of sailing vessels, built the first large wharf in Galveston, and helped the Menard brothers increase the Roman Catholic presence in Texas.

Significant attempts to settle more French on Texas soil did not occur again until the 1840s. The first of those was through the efforts of Henri Castro, a Frenchman of Portuguese and Jewish ancestry who had served as an officer in the French army under Napoleon before coming to America in 1827. After becoming a U.S. citizen, Castro returned to France in 1838 and became a partner in a bank. Tired of banking, his interest in Texas led him to obtain a contract

Henri Castro (1786–1865), empresario and founder of Castro's Colony. Institute of Texan Cultures no. 68-2282

from the government of the Republic of Texas to settle an area southwest of San Antonio with German-speaking immigrants from Alsace, France. By 1847 he had managed to bring 485 families and 457 single men to his land grant along the Medina River where the towns of Castroville (1844), Quihi (1845), Vandenburg (1846), and D'Hanis (1847) were established.

Castro's settlers had to arrive with their own tools and pay thirty-two dollars for the transatlantic passage to Texas. They could not have a criminal record, had to be of good character, and could not sell liquor, gunpowder, or firearms to the Indians. In return, Castro provided transportation to his land grant and allotted each family or single man 640 acres bordering on the Medina River, enough material to build a house, and adequate food to last until a crop could be harvested.

Castroville, the main settlement of the French settlers, faced drought and epidemics during its first years of existence and suffered Indian raids until the 1880s. Head rights issued the first year went mainly to immigrants from the province of Alsace in France. Despite adverse conditions in Texas, these colonists clung to their wilderness homes. They built small stone houses with steeply pitched roofs in the Alsatian style and laid the cornerstone for the St. Louis Catholic Church.

Castroville soon had a brewery, gristmill, cotton gin, and shingle mill as well as stores and a large comfortable inn for weary travelers on the busy road from San Antonio to Del Rio and points west. In 1848 the town became the seat of the newly created Medina County. One traveler in 1857 described the town as "cottages scattered prettily . . . the whole aspect being as far from Texas as possible. It might sit for the portrait of one of the poorer villages of the [Europe's] upper Rhone Valley."[1]

Castro's efforts cost him dearly. Having spent much of his own money to finance the settlement, he was bankrupt by 1845. As a result, he transferred his colonization grant to a group of Belgian businessmen. When returning to France, he died of yellow fever in Monterrey, Mexico.

In contrast to Castroville, La Réunion near Dallas was a different type of mid-nineteenth-century French community. The five hundred people living in La Réunion functioned as a cooperative in which it was necessary to obtain permission from the group before growing, making, and selling food and other goods. Their leader was Victor Considérant, and with him and his French settlers were a small number of Belgians, Swiss, and Germans. They might have succeeded in making their colony a success except most were scientists, artists, musicians, skilled carpenters, or silversmiths with only two experienced farmers in the group. Even so, for a time they survived drought, a plague of grasshoppers, and an icy North Texas winter. Then they began to want to grow and sell what they pleased without having the group vote on such matters. The colony broke up, and by 1856 many of its members had moved to Dallas. There they helped form what became the basis of the fine arts heritage of

the city. Others went to New Orleans or back to France. By 1858 La Réunion no longer existed.

A cabin built in 1857 at La Réunion colony. Courtesy Special Collections, The University of Texas at Arlington Libraries, Arlington, Texas. Institute of Texan Cultures no. 68-2264

The next major influx of French to Texas resulted from the work of the Franco-Texan Land Company. The company secured a number of investors to acquire land in the 1870s in North Texas. They brought over two thousand French immigrants. Most of them became farmers and ranchers and introduced the first draft horses through a breed herd in Albany, Texas.

Regardless of where they settled in Texas during the mid-1800s, most French, like the Menards and Labadie, were Roman Catholics. As a result, with urging from the Menard brothers, the Archdiocese of New Orleans sent Father John Timon as prefect apostolic and Father John M. Odin as vice prefect apostolic to Texas in 1841 to undertake the revitalization of the church. French priests and nuns who established convents, hospitals, churches, orphanages, and schools followed them. The Ursuline Sisters of New Orleans, for example, built schools in Galveston and San Antonio. France's

Mother St. Claire Valentine (1829–98), center, French nun, with others at the convent of the Congregation of the Incarnate Word and Blessed Sacrament in Victoria, Texas, ca. 1890s. Institute of Texan Cultures no. 83-901

Society of Mary Brothers had a school in San Antonio that led to the creation of St. Mary's University. The Incarnate Word Order of Lyons, France, created hospitals in Galveston and San Antonio and later Incarnate Word College in the Alamo City. The Sisters of Divine Providence from Lorraine, France, founded schools in Galveston, Corpus Christi, and Castroville and established what is now Our Lady of the Lake University in San Antonio. All these endeavors, financed mainly from France, provided greatly needed medical, educational, social, and religious services to Texans by the late 1870s.

The French Roman Catholic presence in Texas was well enough established to benefit the next wave of French—the Cajuns. The Cajuns had emigrated from France and settled in Acadia, Nova Scotia, Canada. After England defeated France in the Seven Years' War in 1763 and took possession of Canada, the British, twelve years later, forced out the French Acadians. Some moved to the West Indies, but most went to French-controlled Louisiana instead. When the United States purchased the Louisiana Territory from France in 1803, Acadians living there became American citizens. Over time they became known as "Cadians" and finally "Cajuns."

Between 1900 and 1946 more Louisiana French Cajuns moved to Texas. Especially appealing to them were job opportunities in the

Houston and Golden Triangle (Jefferson County) areas. They worked in shipping, oil refining, and rice production. The Cajuns spoke a language reflective of their heritage with words from French, English, German, Spanish, American Indian, and African American dialects.

Cajuns brought to Texas not only their lively music but also their unique cooking. One well-known dish is *boudain*, "a kind of sausage made of pork, pork liver, cooked rice, and seasonings—parsley, salt, pepper, and the tops of green onions. The boiled meat is put through a sausage mill, mixed with the seasonings and rice, and stuffed into a casing." Like most Cajun dishes, *boudain* calls for rice, a staple of the Cajun diet. Many Cajun recipes end with the words "serve over cooked rice."[2]

Gumbo, too, is an important dish of the Cajuns. One necessary part of gumbo is roux, a sauce or gravy made of fat, flour, onions,

The Butcher family in their buggy at Castroville, ca. 1900s. Institute of Texan Cultures no. 77-49

▼▼▼

19

Cooking barbeque at Castroville. Institute of Texan Cultures no. 72-868

and water. Some Cajuns add a powder made of dried sassafras leaves, called filé, to their gumbo. Jambalaya, along with *boudain* and gumbo, is a favorite dish of the Cajuns. In 1977 W. T. Oliver of Port Arthur, Texas, was using the following recipe to make his favorite Cajun dish:

Cajun Shrimp and Crabmeat Jambalaya

2 pounds cleaned, deveined shrimp
1 cup celery, chopped
2 to 3 garlic cloves, chopped
1 cup green onions, chopped
1 pound crabmeat
salt and pepper
1 cup water
2 cups cooked rice
red pepper to taste

Sauté shrimp, celery, garlic, and onions in a Dutch cast iron oven or large pot until shrimp are about done. Add crabmeat, salt, and pepper. Add 1 cup water and simmer 5 minutes. Add 2 cups cooked rice. Be sure there is enough broth to cover the rice. Mix and simmer together until done—about 10 to 15 minutes. Add plenty of red pepper. Makes 6 to 10 servings.

Traditional French food is not as spicy as the Cajun foods. A favorite recipe passed through Alsace descendants at Castroville is New Year's Bread.

New Year's Bread
1 stick margarine
1 cup sugar
2 eggs
1 envelope of yeast
1 cup warm water
1 cup scalded milk
flour
1 egg, beaten

Cream melted margarine and sugar. Add 2 eggs to the mixture. Dissolve yeast in warm water and add to mixture. Add milk and beat in enough flour to make stiff dough. Set in a warm place and let rise until double in size. Knead and divide into three equal parts and braid. The braid may be placed on a flat baking sheet in a long loaf or joined to form a wreath. Let rise again. Brush with a beaten egg and bake at 350° for about 1 hour. Makes one loaf.

Such foods from the French Texans are an essential part of their celebrations. Castroville's honoring of its patron St. Louis at its Catholic church features their famous Alsatian sausage. Another special day is Bastille Day on July 14 that signals the beginning of the French

Revolution of 1789. Equally important is Port Arthur's Cajun Crawfish Festival held in May. Whatever the occasion, for the more than 571,175 (1990).[3] Texans of French descent, all such events offer a grand opportunity to portray for others their unique culture.

THE ENGLISH TEXANS

1870: 2,090
1890: 9,443
1900: 8,213
1910: 8,498

Lillie Barr Munroe was the daughter of an English mother, Amelia Barr, and a Scottish father, Robert Barr. As a young girl, Lillie came with her family to Texas from England in 1856. They settled in Austin where Lillie's father worked as a secretary with the Texas legislature.

Although her parents opposed slavery, they supported the Confederacy during the American Civil War. Lillie, however, was not as patriotic to the Southern cause as is evident in her recollection of events leading up to a dinner given by Austin city fathers for Confederate General John Magruder.

> Some citizens of Austin looked all over the city for turkeys. I had a lovely turkey hen named Nellie. I had raised her from a chick. I had fed her out of my plate until she was grown. I loved that turkey as a boy loves a dog. They came to Mother's and bought all of her turkeys, Nellie among them. I was away at the time. When I came home and found my Nellie gone, I was terribly unhappy. Mother thought I would be proud to give my pet for so brave a soldier. Not I. I went into the fields and prayed to God. If that man ate my Nellie to let a bone to choke him and if he went back to the war, to let some Yankees to kill him with a bayonet. Most likely he never tasted my Nellie, but he was the cause of her being killed. He may have been a good soldier, but my Nellie stood between me and him.[4]

▼▼▼

Amelia E. Barr (1831–1919), a fashionable Austin resident, November, 1880. Institute of Texan Cultures no. 75-1241

Lillie, a few years earlier, had heard her parents talk about Great Britain as their "home." Lillie had been so used to being in Texas that she was surprised to realize that she and her parents "were not Texas born."

The Barr family was typical of English immigrants who came to Texas during the 1850s. They found institutions similar to the ones

▼▼▼

they had left behind. Speaking the English language only with a different accent and finding representative government, Protestant churches, and a system of common law that they were familiar with, they quickly assimilated into the Anglo-American majority from the United States. Assimilation began with the first English to settle in Texas. Some were part of *empresario* efforts by Englishmen John Charles Beales's Rio Grande project in 1833 and William S. Peters's colony in North Texas during 1841. Another early arrival, Charles Stanfield Taylor, a Nacogdoches merchant, was a signer of the Texas Declaration of Independence.

The majority of the English, however, arrived in Texas after the 1840s. They came for a variety of reasons. In England, second or later sons could not inherit property from their father. By law, the estate and lands went to the eldest son. Younger males in the family had to seek their fortunes elsewhere, and those from well-to-do Anglican families had the money to make the journey to Texas. Workers in more modest families, usually Presbyterians, Methodists, or Baptists, who lived in crowded cities, had trouble finding well-paying jobs. They and the even poorer farmers in England not only had to pay high taxes but also could not afford to purchase property.

Texas offered new hope to such people. In the mid-1800s one could buy a 640-acre section of undeveloped Texas prairie land for as little as five dollars an acre—a price unbelievable in England. English immigrants quickly took advantage of such land opportunities. Most succeeded while enduring drought and hostile Indians. As a result, some helped to make farming a mainstay on the western prairies of Texas.

Other English were interested in large-scale cattle, sheep, and goat ranching in West Texas. The largest such endeavor was the famous XIT Ranch. The Capitol Freehold Land and Investment Company of London purchased the ranch from a Chicago firm and began surveying the acreage in 1884. It covered ten counties in the Texas Panhandle. The Texas legislature sold the three-million-acre ranch to the English company to pay for the cost of building the

Frank Collinson (1855–1943), an English buffalo hunter and rancher. Institute of Texan Cultures no. 68-2435

state capitol building in Austin. The XIT owners remained in England while local Texans managed the huge ranch. It was through the efforts of large British-owned ranches that barbed wire, electric fences, steel windmills, deep wells, and dipping vats were introduced into northwest Texas. Also, after much experimentation with cattle on the British Isles to maximize the amount of beef per cow, purebred Herefords were sent to the Panhandle in 1879.

The class society of England did present issues for some of the arriving aristocracy who saw Texans as ignorant and crude. Texans in turn saw those English as arrogant and helpless. One of the most colorful English owners was Heneage Finch, the Seventh Earl of Aylesford, who "arrived in Big Spring in 1883 after leaving England to escape a disastrous divorce scandal. Setting himself up as a small rancher, he bought the local hotel in order that he or his guests would always have a room when needed; he bought a local butcher shop so

Joseph Heneage Finch, Seventh Earl of Aylesford (1849–85), pictured in 1883 about the time he arrived in Texas. Institute of Texan Cultures no. 68-2437

▼▼▼

he would always have meat cut to his liking; and he bought the saloon to ensure a ready supply of whiskey, a half gallon a day."[5]

Unlike Heneage Finch, most of the English immigrants, like Lillie Barr, quickly adapted to life in Texas. In the process, they settled across the state, entering into all occupations. This second-largest European immigrant group in Texas during the nineteenth century easily assimilated, experiencing neither the prejudice nor the biased sentiment aimed at some other groups. The extent to which they assimilated is evident in the lives of some notable English Texans such as David Richardson, a journalist who arrived in Texas during 1852 and created the *Texas Almanac* so familiar to most readers today. Another English immigrant, William J. Marsh, coauthored "Texas, Our Texas," the state anthem, in 1929.

Equally significant was the work of Rabbi Henry Cohen. During 1888 Rabbi Cohen, an English Jew, settled in Galveston. He quickly became a leader in the fight for social justice. He served as a chief spokesperson for the welfare of the poor, the unemployed, and the sick. He worked for better facilities to help those in prison and to acquire equal rights for all people. He also eased the way for immigrants from many countries, including Russia, as they tried to learn the new language and find jobs.

While becoming Texans, the English left their distinctive British mark on Texas through the naming of a few dust-blown cow towns such as Tennyson, Wellington, Clarendon, Salisbury, Hereford, and others. They also managed to preserve some aspects of their native culture, including their unique foods. The great-grandmother of Mrs. Bill Early from Big Spring, Texas, brought this recipe and story from England in 1846 and on to Texas in 1887—a special favorite for the more than 2,024,001 (1990)[6] Texans of English descent.

English Poor Folks Plum Pudding
An English Lord, having had a very bad year of drought, was worried as to what he could feed the serfs for a Christmas feast. He ordered his cooks to find something—anything—and the following is the recipe as it came to America. Equal

Rabbi Henry Cohen (1863–1952) with wife, Molly Levy, and family. Institute of Texan Cultures no. 68-2531

parts of raisins, currants, suet. Enough flour and water to make it stick together. Mix and stuff tightly into small sacks; tie lightly; boil for about 3 hours. Let cool thoroughly. Cut into thin slices; heat through; serve with sauce. Make a thin flour starch sauce; add enough sugar, nutmeg, and butter to taste good; serve over heated pudding.

With this as a guide, the family worked out the following recipe, which puts the finishing touch to their Christmas dinners:

1 pound raisins
1 teaspoon salt
2 to 3 cups flour
1 pound currants
1 cup cold water
1 pound suet, finely chopped

Mix ingredients together. Scald two small flour sacks. Flour them well. Pack pudding tightly into small sacks and tie. Place sacks on a rack "just off the bottom" of a large kettle of boiling water. Boil 3 hours. More boiling water may be added if necessary. Let age 1 to 2 weeks. To serve: Remove from sack. Slice into pieces ⅓ to ½ inch thick. Heat in oven until suet is clear and pudding is hot. Serve with sauce.

Sauce:
1 cup sugar
1 teaspoon flour
2 to 3 cups boiling water
1 tablespoon butter
1 teaspoon salt
1 teaspoon nutmeg
1 teaspoon vanilla (optional)

Mix dry ingredients. Add the remaining ingredients and boil well. Serve hot over the warm slices of pudding.

THE SCOTTISH TEXANS

1870: 620
1890: 2,172
1900: 1,952
1910: 2,038

The story of the Scots in Texas is one of individuals rather than groups of Scots forming communities. Scots were well represented among the numerous Europeans who joined the Texas Revolution against Mexican dictator Santa Anna in the 1830s. John MacGregor, born in Scotland, was among the rebelling Texans that drove the Mexican army from San Antonio in the winter of 1835. He served as a cannoneer, or gunner, and as a second sergeant several months later during the siege of the Alamo. Legend has it that as a bagpiper he played along while David Crockett played the fiddle, entertaining troops garrisoned at the Alamo in the days prior to the fall of the mission on March 6, 1836.

A tribute to the bravery shown by John MacGregor's stand at the Alamo came from Zoe Alexander:

The Last Warrior Piper
That 'neath Texas blue-bonnets lies a Scot?
That a Child of the Mist saw our freedom was bought?
For MacGregor was there to pipe in the new State,
And as Pipers of old, he went proud to his fate.
He stood with his brothers, disdaining to flee,
Blowing up the warpipes as he gazed o'er the sea
Of the Mexican army, who'd never heard the squall
Of the bagpipes, nor knew the Celtic war call. . . .
And the wrongs of the ages rode hard on his back,
As the cannons roared out Santa Anna's attack.
Now the warpipe lies silent, unmarked in his grave. . . .[7]

Neil McLennan (1777–1867), a Scottish immigrant to Central Texas by way of North Carolina and Florida, ca. 1835. Institute of Texan Cultures no. 68-2804

▼▼▼

John MacGregor was one among the Scots who died defending the Alamo. Others included David L. Wilson, Isaac Robinson, and Richard Ballentine, all in their youthful twenties. The Cameron clan also joined in the battles of the Texas Revolution. John Cameron arrived in 1827 and also fought in the 1835 siege of Bexar. Ewen Cameron came in 1835 and fought at the battle of San Jacinto on April 21, 1836. He went on to serve under numerous leaders and was taken prisoner at the battle of Mier. Luckily, he drew a white bean in the Black Bean Episode and escaped death, only to be shot later when he attempted to escape from another Mexican imprisonment. Another member of the clan, William Cameron, did not fight in any battles, but by the late 1860s was a well-to-do businessman in Waco.

Among the other Scots to arrive in Texas was Neil McLennan. McLennan came to Texas in 1839 and surveyed the area that is now McLennan County. The three-hundred-thousand-acre Matador

Ranch hands on the Matador Cattle Company, ca. 1883. Institute of Texan Cultures no. 68-2820

▼▼▼

Scottish stonecutters cutting granite for the state capitol in Austin. Institute of Texan Cultures no. 68-810

Cattle Company in West Texas was financed with money from Scotland, and Scotsman Murdo Mackenzie came as manager.

By the late 1880s William Menzies was not only a cattle rancher but also a pioneer sheepman. Thomas Affleck started one of the early nurseries in Texas and became an authority on the state's agriculture. Robert Bontine Cunninghame Graham came to Texas in 1879 with his young wife hoping to become a cattle king. He lost his capital and became a cowboy instead, traveling the west while trying out his writing skills. He became one of the state's first folklorists.

Sixty-five stonecutters from Aberdeen, Scotland, also arrived in Texas during 1882. Their presence in Texas created some dissension. A labor union protested that the Scottish stonecutters were immigrant laborers who worked for less pay than the native-born artisans. After U.S. President Benjamin Harrison intervened, the Scots were allowed to practice their trade. By 1886 they had completed their excellent granite work for the state's new capitol building.

One of the first Scottish Presbyterian preachers in Texas was John McCullough. In 1840 he established the First Presbyterian Church of Galveston. Six years later, he founded the First Presbyterian Church of San Antonio.

Scattered throughout the state, the Scots decided to do something about retaining their old-world traditions. In the mid–twentieth century they began to celebrate the "Gathering of the Clans" at Salado, located between Waco and Austin in southern Bell County, and during November hold "Highland Games" such as the one held during the spring at McLennan Community College in Waco.

Based on the older contests dating from the 1700s in Scotland, the Texas Highland Games, with men dressed in kilts, highlight a variety of events. There is the "skir-r-rling o' the bagpipes" and con-

A bust of Scottish physician Edmund Duncan Montgomery (1835–1911), husband of German sculptress Elisabet Ney (1833–1907). Institute of Texan Cultures no. 68-2815

A Scotsman in his traditional clan dress with bagpipe. Institute of Texan Cultures no. 68-2829

tests of dancing and physical strength. At one time, Scots used the bagpipe not only for musical entertainment but also as a weapon in war. During a battle, the nondirectional sound from the bagpipe signaled troop movement and made it very difficult for the enemy to identify its location. At other times, the bagpiper led the Scottish troops into battle.

▼▼▼

Scottish games of physical strength include tossing the caber and sheaf. The caber looks like a small telephone pole. According to the competition rules,

men's caber is to be a maximum of 17' and a minimum of 15'. Approximate weight shall not be over 100 pounds and not less than 80 pounds to start. . . . In no case will anyone be allowed more than three tosses at any one length. The caber may be carried to the pickup point by another person and the small end may be braced by another person while being raised. No further assistance may be had. Competitor must raise, balance, and lift caber alone. Caber shall be tossed for straightness only; distance is not to be considered. A full turn end for end in straight line is the perfect toss and each turn is to be awarded 100 points. . . .

The sheaf can be a 16-pound bale of hay or a sackcloth bag filled with straw. The goal is for one to use a pitchfork to continue to toss the bale over a horizontal bar. With each successful toss, judges raise the bar an inch higher. If two or more contestants successfully toss the sheaf over the highest point, the judges lower the bar and use a heavier bale of hay. The contest then continues until there is a winner.[8]

And, what would any Highland Game be without traditional Scottish foods? Clottie Dumplin is a Scottish pudding, and black bun is a New Year's Eve fruitcake that can also be served for breakfast. Prepared according to traditional recipes for the more than 36,854 (1990)[9] Texans of Scottish descent, Clottie Dumplin requires the following:

Scottish Clottie Dumplin
2 cups sifted flour
2 cups dry bread crumbs
½ teaspoon ginger
1 teaspoon cinnamon
1 cup finely chopped suet
1 teaspoon baking soda

1 cup raisins, chopped
1 or 2 eggs (optional)
½ cup currants
1 to 1½ cups buttermilk or ale
¾ cup sugar
sugar for dredging

Mix flour, bread crumbs, suet, raisins, currants, sugar, ginger, cinnamon, and soda together in a bowl. Beat in the eggs and add one cup of buttermilk or ale. Mix to form a soft dough. Add more liquid, if necessary. Dip a large pudding cloth in boiling water and wring it out. Set inside a bowl and dust with flour. Spoon the batter into the cloth. Tie the cloth tightly at the top, leaving room for pudding to swell. Place cloth in a large pot, such as a cast iron Dutch oven, and set on a rack, with an upturned saucer placed on top for a lid. Cover with boiling water. Simmer for 2 ½ hours. Lift the pudding out and put on a plate in oven to dry for a few minutes. Dredge with sugar and serve. Makes 10 to 12 servings. To use leftover pudding, cut into slices, squeeze with lemon juice, fry in hot butter, and dredge with sugar. (Cheesecloth may be substituted for pudding cloth.)

Scottish Black Bun
This is the traditional Hogmanay (New Year's Eve) fruitcake.

Crust:
½ teaspoon baking powder
3 cups flour
½ cup butter
½ teaspoon salt
1 egg, beaten

Sift flour, salt, and baking powder. Cut in butter until mixture is like coarse meal. Mix in egg. If necessary, add a few drops of cold water to make dough. Roll out pastry on a lightly floured board. Line large, greased loaf pans or baking dishes with pastry, retaining enough dough to make tops.

Cake:
1 teaspoon ginger
4 cups flour
¼ teaspoon cloves
2 cups currants
1 teaspoon pepper
2 cups raisins
1 teaspoon baking soda
1 cup almonds, chopped
1 cup milk
1 cup mixed chopped peel
2 tablespoons brandy or sherry
2 teaspoons cinnamon
1 egg, beaten

Sift flour into large bowl. Mix in currants, raisins, almonds, peel, cinnamon, ginger, cloves, pepper, and baking soda. Blend in milk and brandy. Turn into pastry-lined pans. Flatten surface. Put on a pastry lid or top and crimp edges together. Poke four holes to the bottom of the pan with a skewer. Pierce the top surface all over with a fork. Brush crust with beaten egg. Bake at 350° for 3 hours if one large cake; reduce the time if cake is smaller.

▼▼▼

THE IRISH TEXANS

1870: 4,144
1890: 8,201
1900: 6,173
1910: 5,357

Saint Patrick's Day, March 17, celebrates the patron saint of Ireland. It is a day to wear green, display shamrocks, look for leprechauns, and play pennywhistles as well as to tell tall tales. The Irish are famous for their stories. One tells how Irish fairies—the "wee folk"— came to Texas. Mike Welch, a well-known Irish Texan storyteller in the early 1900s, would begin his tale with a rumor that his house in Texas was haunted.

It's not haunted, exactly. One might have noticed that this house is in a flat area surrounded by sort of a wide ditch. The ditch isn't very plain any more, but if you had ever lived in Ireland, as I have, you'd realize that it isn't a ditch at all. It's an old moat. You see, many years ago in Ireland, every castle was surrounded by a moat. My house here is built in the center where an old castle had stood. I guess you are wondering how such things as a moat and a castle came to be in Texas.

Well, it was the work of fairies. A long time ago in Ireland, there was a kind and wealthy man who was a good friend of the fairy folk. He had a good and beautiful daughter, and when she was old enough to marry, it was arranged for her to marry the son of an Irish lord.

An English baron who lived nearby also wanted to marry the girl, but he was turned down. The baron was determined to steal the girl away, but the castle was too well protected for him to attack openly.

On May Eve, when the wedding feast was in full swing, and the guards at the castle were drunk with too much wine, the baron and his men broke into the castle and killed the revelers. The young couple that was walking in the garden in the moonlight at the time of the attack did not escape. The lad was cut down as he defended his bride. She, seeing him die, plunged his sword into her own body so she might die with him. When morning came, the castle was in ruins, and the moat flowed red with blood.

When the fairies saw what had happened, they begged God to restore the castle just as it had been before the slaughter. God offered to restore the castle and the people only if the fairies would carry them away to where no Irish would ever see them. The fairies picked up the castle, moat and all, and carried it across the ocean to this unknown world and set it down in Texas.

Then the New World was discovered. It wasn't long until people began to come to Texas, the Irish among them. The fairies had promised that the castle would not be seen by Irish eyes; so they caused the castle to sink into the earth completely. Only the outlines of the moat were left. That is the way I found it when I came here. . . .[10]

The Irish brought more than tales to Texas. They were among the first settlers in Spanish-ruled Texas. The earliest ones included Hugo Oconór, an interim governor of Spanish Texas during the late 1700s. Philip Nolan of Belfast, Ireland, made four expeditions into Texas from his home in New Orleans. He was a mustanger trapping wild horses for the Louisiana military. On one expedition he returned with twelve hundred mustangs. The Spanish were not happy with his forays into Texas from the United States, and in 1801 Spanish troops from Nacogdoches were sent to capture him. Nolan was killed and his men taken prisoner.

Between 1815 and 1845 four Irish *empresarios*, John McMullen, James McGloin, James Power, and James Hewetson, settled the two Irish colonies of San Patricio and Refugio in South Texas. The original settlers emigrated from affluent areas in Ireland and had the means to pay for their voyage to Texas plus provide a year's provisions. The better-off tenant farmers looked to escape the overpopulation of the countryside and to buy their own land in Texas. Some Irish came as merchants, but they all came hoping to acquire land and improve their lives.[11]

Reverend Mother Margaret Mary Healy-Murphy (1833–1907)

Margaret Mary Healy was born in County Kerry, Ireland. After the death of her mother, she came with her father and relatives to West Virginia in 1839. Her father, a doctor, died while taking the family to Texas, but Margaret and her relatives continued on to Matamoros where Margaret assisted her aunts in operating a hotel.

At sixteen she married John B. Murphy, also from Ireland, who was a volunteer in General Taylor's army. In 1850 they settled in Corpus Christi where he was a lawyer and ranch owner. Margaret Healy-Murphy began offering help to the sick, poor, and uneducated children and in 1875 along with three friends

Members of the Irish community gather following Sunday Mass near Gussettville, Texas, ca. 1909–12. Institute of Texan Cultures no. 79-183

The Irish were everywhere in Texas. Father Michael Muldoon, an Irish Roman Catholic priest, worked with settlers in Stephen F. Austin's colony. Four Irish Texans signed the Texas Declaration of Independence on March 2, 1836. Fourteen Irish immigrants were part of James Fannin's army killed by Mexican troops at Goliad. Over one hundred Irishmen were in Sam Houston's forces when they defeated Santa Anna's army at San Jacinto. Irishwoman Peggy McCormick owned the land on which they fought the battle. Shortly after the fighting ended, Peggy could be heard complaining about the smell of the dead Mexican soldiers.

Large-scale immigration by the Irish to Texas occurred as the Republic of Texas was formed. These Irish came for different rea-

Reverend Mother Margaret Mary Healy-Murphy (1833–1907). Institute of Texan Cultures no. 74-1175

purchased a center for the homeless that became known as "Mrs. Murphy's hospital for the poor." After the death of John in 1884, Margaret worked full time and used her financial resources to purchase property in San Antonio to build a church, convent, and school, which offered hospital care and education to all people regardless of race or religion. In 1888 she opened the first school for African Americans in San Antonio.

In 1892, fifteen years before her death, she became the Reverend Mother Margaret Mary Healy-Murphy and established the Sisters of the Holy Ghost, the first religious order founded in Texas. Today, the Sisters of the Holy Ghost have thirty-nine missions in Texas, Louisiana, and Mississippi to help the poor and those

sons. The English who controlled Ireland ruled that only members of the Protestant Anglican Church could hold public office. That left out the Irish, most of whom were Roman Catholics along with a minority of Presbyterians. The English also seized properties of members of the Irish ruling class, denied the Irish an education, and forced many of the Irish farmers into poverty by levying high

▼▼▼

in need of educational assistance.

Source: John Brendan Flannery, *The Irish Texans* (San Antonio: Institute of Texans Cultures, 1980) pp. 129–32.

taxes. Then came a massive potato crop failure caused by a blight that hit Ireland from 1845 to 1850. While people starved, landlords evicted over five hundred thousand tenant farmers who could not pay their rents. Meanwhile, England exported livestock and tons of grain from Ireland. The 1850 census listed 1,403 Irish in Texas; ten years later the number was 3,480.

The first group who managed to survive the horrible conditions aboard ship went to live on several Texas land grants. Mostly Roman Catholics, the Irish settled in the Austin colony created by *empresario* Stephen F. Austin. Others went to colonies created in Refugio County by James Hewetson and James Power, a signer of the Texas Declaration of Independence, or to the one settled by John McMullen and James McGloin in San Patricio County. Those that were Presbyterians settled in Robertson County. Still others went to San Antonio where they worked as day laborers. Those arriving in the 1870s and 1880s found employment in Houston, while others labored to build railroads in Texas.

A few Irish Texans kept general merchandising stores or taught in the schools. However, as was true for most people living in Texas during the 1820s through the 1850s, the Irish were mainly farmers or ranchers. Daily life in the rural Irish communities was difficult.

Staples were bacon, jerked beef, coffee and corn cakes, when the corn could be milled. Hand mills were at first used for grinding corn. Before grinding, the corn was thrown on hot embers to drive out the weevils, then husked in lye. . . . Game was plentiful in Texas, and the meals included venison, wild turkey, and squirrel. Soon small vegetable gardens and fruit trees added to the fare. Water was supplied by wells or from nearby creeks. . . .

Cabin-style houses were built of logs with floors of smoothed boards. . . . Those who did not have such a handy source of planks could purchase boards from the commercial houses on the coast. Inland, where rocks could be dug from the hillsides, stone houses were built. . . . When the Indians were still a threat, the settlers often constructed a small brush pen or corral at the rear of the house,

with no entrance except that provided by the rear of the dwelling. When Indians were known to be in the neighborhood, the milk cows, oxen, and saddle horses were driven through the house into this pen.

Herds of mustangs . . . roamed the plains. These, the settlers attempted to tame. They would first capture one, place a stuffed dummy on his back, and then set him loose. The horse would attempt to rejoin the herd. . . .

A gathering at the home of Mary and Thomas McGuill near Blanconia with Dr. J. J. Adkins holding a broom. Institute of Texan Cultures no. 79-308

▼▼▼

43

A tournament knight in the backyard of the Coniziene Heard residence in Refugio, Texas, ca. 1905. Institute of Texan Cultures no. 82-610

The children of the family had the chores usual to those living on a farm or ranch. The girls learned to cook, launder, sew, embroider, and look after the house. The boys helped in farming, caring for the livestock, and hunting and trapping wild animals. While still in their teens, most children had to assume adult responsibilities. . . .[12]

Along with weddings, anniversaries, and birthdays, other celebrations played an important role in the lives of the Irish. One old-timer described a Fourth of July celebration in Refugio County that included

▼▼▼

a tournament in the morning . . . a big free barbecue at noon . . . the afternoon devoted to horse racing, and a big dance at night.

The tournament was a competition in which horsemen vied with each other in spearing rings from eight posts spaced at 40-foot intervals. Each rider carried a six-foot to eight-foot pike sharpened at the end and, with this under his arm, rode full tilt for the rings. He was scored on the number of rings speared and the elapsed time on the course.[13]

The McGuill General Store with family members on the porch in Blanconia, Texas, ca. 1904. Institute of Texan Cultures illustration no. 79-84

Living under such harsh conditions did not deter the Irish Texans. They persevered, and their descendants would continue to settle throughout the state. In the process, they entered and succeeded in every field of endeavor. A few entered the field of journalism. For example, lawyer and surveyor Dr. Francis Moore became editor of the *Telegraph and Texas Register,* the leading newspaper in Texas during the 1830s and 1840s. In the area of higher education, Presbyterian Samuel McKinney was one of the early presidents of Austin College.

Irish Texans also contributed to the culinary specialties of Texas. Some of those enjoyed by the 572,732 (1980)[14] Texans of Irish descent and others include the following:

Irish Beef and Potatoes O' Blarney
8 small minute steaks
¼ chopped onion
1 cup water
2 tablespoons celery flakes
2 tablespoons butter
2 tablespoons parsley flakes
½ teaspoon salt
1 teaspoon basil, crushed
⅓ cup milk
½ teaspoon rosemary, crushed
1½ cups mashed potato flakes
¼ teaspoon pepper
1 egg, slightly beaten
¼ pound butter

Season steaks as desired. In a saucepan, bring water with butter and salt to boiling. Remove from heat and add milk. Stir in potato flakes, let stand until soft and moist, and then whip lightly. Add remainder of the ingredients, except butter, and mix well. Place a spoonful of the potato mixture on the edge of each steak. Roll loosely and fasten with toothpicks. Melt ¼ pound butter in a shallow baking pan. Roll each steak in the butter and place in the pan. Bake at 350° for 55 minutes, turning occasionally. Makes 8 servings.

Irish Boxty

Boxty is a traditional potato dish that resembles griddle cakes or potato pancakes that is served on Halloween in Ireland.

1 pound potatoes
salt and pepper
1 teaspoon baking soda
2 cups cooked mashed potatoes
½ cup melted butter
4 cups flour
enough milk to make a batter

Peel the raw potatoes and grate. Squeeze out the liquid in a clean tea towel and keep. Mix the liquid with the mashed potatoes. Add grated potatoes. Add flour, salt, pepper, baking soda, butter, and enough milk or potato water to make a batter. Grease a skillet and cook pancakes over moderate heat. Boxty is served with butter and sometimes sprinkled with sugar.

THE DUTCH TEXANS

1870: 54
1890: 130
1900: 262
1910: 424

An early Dutch arrival in Texas was Felipe Enrique Neri. He left Holland after being accused of stealing money that he had supposedly collected as a tax collector. In 1795 he made his way to Spanish Louisiana and renamed himself Baron de Bastrop. When Louisiana was sold to the United States, he moved to San Antonio and started a freighting business. In 1810 he worked as second *alcalde* (assistant to the mayor) in the town government and as a land merchant, a job in which he was not very successful. In 1820 he helped Moses Austin and later his son, Stephen, to obtain the legal rights to establish their colony in Texas. Bastrop intervened with both the Spanish and then the Mexican authorities to allow Moses and Stephen to establish a settlement. He continued to represent Texas through his work as an elected official in the provincial capital of Saltillo. Bastrop worked to establish legislation favorable to immigration and the interests of settlers and was also central in the passage of an act establishing a port at Galveston that opened the way for more immigrants to enter Texas. As the result of his efforts, thousands of people with varying cultures were able to move to Texas.

Aside from Bastrop, only a few others from Holland arrived during the 1830s through the 1870s. David Levi Kokernot, a Dutch Jew, fought in the Texas Revolution of 1835 and 1836. He later served as a Texas Ranger, fought for the Confederacy during the American Civil War, and became a successful rancher near Fort Davis in West Texas. Kokernot Field at Sul Ross University in Alpine is named for his family. Another Dutchman, Vincentian priest John Brands, strengthened the Roman Catholic Church in the Galveston area during the 1840s. In 1877 William Henry Snyder began a settlement near his trading post, and the town that developed now bears his surname.

This slow trickle of Dutch immigrants to Texas changed in the 1880s. Land investors began to bring in Dutch families, but the attempts failed. In Denton County, crop failures caused its inhabitants to move away. The town of Gothland in Brazoria County also ended when the great hurricane of 1900 destroyed the town. Theodore Koch sponsored a third attempt in the coastal area of southeast Texas. In 1900 he convinced a number of Dutch families, mostly from Iowa, to move to Winnie, Texas. There they bought land from Koch for forty dollars an acre. They called their town New Holland. At first they did well, raising cabbage, cucumbers, melons, and potatoes, but their prosperity did not last. A severe hurricane with a ten-foot tidal wave in 1910 destroyed their crops. As a result, seventy-seven of the eighty families left Texas, and New Holland became a ghost town.

The Port Arthur Land Company built the Orange Hotel in Nederland where new arrivals from Holland stayed until their homes were built, ca. 1898. Institute of Texan Cultures illustration no. 72-982

The most successful Dutch colony in Texas began in 1897 as a result of Dutch investors forming the Port Arthur Land Company. They began to sell plots from sixty-six thousand acres to Dutch immigrants who bought the land for the very low price of eight dollars an acre. Most of the settlers came from Holland where land was too expensive to purchase, while a few Dutch farmers came from South Africa to avoid the military draft.

Located seven miles southeast of Beaumont in eastern Jefferson County, the settlement became known as Nederland. George Rienstra was the first Dutch settler to arrive in November, 1897. Others followed shortly thereafter, and to help the families get settled, the Port Arthur Land Company built the Orange Hotel. It was painted bright orange in honor of the Dutch monarchy of the House of Orange (not a building, but a royal family). The hotel served as temporary living quarters for the immigrants until their homes could be built.

While building their homes, the settlers in Nederland formed a congregation of the Dutch Reformed Church and held services at the Orange Hotel. Although their children attended public school

▼▼▼

The town of Nederland had a wooden sidewalk that helped the pedestrians stay out of the mud or dust in the street, ca. 1903. Institute of Texan Cultures illustration no. 85-121

classes taught in English, church services were in Dutch. Only when the children began to speak more English than Dutch did the congregation conduct services in English. Nevertheless, at mealtime children had to say the following prayer in Dutch: *Heer, zegen deze spys en drank.* Amen. (Lord, bless this food and drink. Amen.)

The Nederland Dutch began to prosper in their occupations. Most became rice farmers, truck farmers, or dairy owners. The depression of 1907 wiped out the rice farmers, but an economic boom began in Beaumont after the discovery of oil at nearby Spindletop in 1901. It allowed the Nederland Dutch to sell their farm products to those in the petroleum industry. Others got jobs with the oil companies.[15]

No matter what their occupations, the hardworking Dutch Texans had a reputation for being very frugal (tight) with their money. They tried to pay cash for all purchases and were careful about being paid for their work. In a story told by the descendants of the Dan Rienstra family, Dick, one of Dan's sons, claims he

▼▼▼

worked for a week or two for a local man. He was supposed to get ten dollars for the work. The man paid him in one-dollar bills. When Dick got home, he re-counted the money. To his surprise, he found only eight dollars! The man had folded over two of the one-dollar bills. Each one looked like two when you just counted the ends. Dick did not rush back and complain that he had been cheated. He bided his time. Years later, Dick went into business. One day his former employer came in and bought something. Dick pulled the same trick when he gave the man his change. The man had not recalled the earlier episode. He was indignant and complained, 'Hey, Dick, you don't know how to count!' Dick replied, 'Oh, yes, I do. You taught me!' Then the man remembered the earlier incident, and they both enjoyed the joke."[16]

Not so humorous to the Nederland Dutch were problems with the almost year-round warm climate of the humid, swamplike southeast Texas coast. The mosquitoes posed an irritating problem. The Nederland Dutch tried many ways to rid themselves of the pesky

Plowing rice levees with mule teams near Nederland, Texas, ca. 1906. Institute of Texan Cultures illustration no. 72-1658

Wedding portrait of Johanna and Dan Rienstra taken in Beaumont, Texas, January 21, 1903. Institute of Texan Cultures illustration no. 72-979

insects. When worshipping, they burned smudge pots outside the church building. This kept the waiting horses from getting bitten so badly. Girls going to picnics or dances wrapped newspapers beneath their stockings to avoid bites. Worse than mosquitoes though were the many alligators, wolves, and poisonous snakes—any one of which could cause death.

The local climate was also the subject of a story about Dan Rienstra. Before he left Holland, he had been told that Texas had such warm temperatures he could comfortably go barefoot outside on Christmas Day. He doubted that and brought his ice skates with him. During his first winter in Nederland, the temperature dropped to two degrees below zero. Dan ice-skated on the Neches River.[17]

As time passed, the Dutch of Nederland became more Americanized. All members of the second generation and thereafter spoke English as their primary language. By the third generation, most spoke little if any Dutch. They also more often married non-Dutch spouses. Some moved elsewhere in search of new jobs. Additionally, the oil boom in the area and the opening of the many refineries associated with it brought in other people who outnumbered the original Dutch settlers and their descendants, changing the ethnic culture of the town.

To revive aspects of their old-world culture, the descendants of the Nederland Dutch built a three-story windmill museum in the city during the 1970s. It preserved artifacts and articles about the town's early history. The Nederland Dutch also included some of their ethnic recipes. Aside from their staple of potatoes and cheeses, they have kept alive the New Year's celebration by eating *olie koeken*. It is like a doughnut with an apple center.

The first law officer in Nederland was Constable Ernest Singleton, left, *with son Dillard,* right, *ca. 1902. Institute of Texan Cultures illustration no. 72-1666*

▼▼▼

There are 202,566 Texans who claim Dutch ancestry, and many still follow the Dutch tradition of eating about six times a day.[18] For a hardworking family, the sequence of meals usually went as follows:

Real Dutch Pancakes

Breakfast is a cold meal of bread, butter, and jam or perhaps cheese and cold meats. Tea, milk, or buttermilk is the usual beverage. Children are often served hot pap (a soft infant food) or cooked cereal. On special occasions, pancakes might be served. Each pancake is usually as big as a dinner plate.

1 cup flour
⅛ teaspoon salt
1 cup milk
2 large eggs, beaten
¼ cup butter or margarine

Put the flour and salt in a bowl, make a well in the middle, and add the beaten eggs. Mix to smooth batter. Add the milk. Melt half the butter in a heavy skillet. Pour in the batter. Turn pancakes frequently, each time adding more butter. They should be golden brown and crisp at the edges. Makes about 6 pancakes.

At ten or eleven in the morning, depending on how early breakfast took place, coffee is served with spice cake or perhaps bread and cheese.

▼▼▼

Dutch Spice Cake
2 cups self-rising flour
1 teaspoon cloves
1 teaspoon cinnamon
½ cup dark brown sugar
1 teaspoon ginger
⅓ cup molasses
½ teaspoon nutmeg
1 cup milk
pinch of salt

Combine all ingredients and beat until smooth. Grease an 8" x 12" cake pan and add batter. Bake at 300° for about 1 hour. Keep in the pan for 24 hours before serving.

Buttered slices of the cake are often served with coffee, or a slice of this cake may be put on a slice of bread and served for breakfast. Makes about 24 slices.

Lunch is another cold meal consisting of liver sausage, ham, or other cold cuts. Dutch rusks (hard, toasted, crisp bread) or different kinds of rolls may be topped with cheese or jam. If there are guests, a hot dish, such as croquettes or an omelet, may be added. Fruit is often served at lunch. The drink is likely to be coffee, milk, buttermilk, or cocoa.

Four o'clock is teatime. A cup of tea, a biscuit, cookies, or a piece of cake is the usual fare. The children are home from school and hungry for a snack, of course.

Dinner is served about seven in the evening and is usually the only hot meal of the day. It typically includes a hot soup followed by meat or fish with vegetables and potatoes. The meal is finished with fruit or perhaps dessert. Coffee may be served with the meal, but generally it is served afterward.

At bedtime, the Dutch prepare coffee or tea. When guests are present, cake might also be served. Otherwise, a cookie or biscuit will do. The Dutch are known for their fine hospitality.

THE BELGIAN TEXANS

1870: 73
1890: 216
1900: 244
1910: 328

In 1842, young Anton Diedrick was walking the streets of his native Antwerp in Belgium when he witnessed a murder. The killers, fearing exposure, had Anton ambushed and put on the first ship going to sea. He remained a virtual prisoner for several years aboard ship until in Galveston he got his chance to go ashore. He had a hard time finding food and a job because he spoke only Flemish, the major language of Belgium. A pair of soldiers recruiting for service in the Mexican War attempted to convince Diedrick that he only had to make his mark and he would be fed and cared for. When asked his name he did not know what they were saying. At last one soldier said in exasperation, "Aw, he's Dutch all over. We'll call him that." Thus, he was listed on the roll as Diedrick Dutchallover. The name was still too cumbersome, so the "all" was dropped, leaving Dutchover.

After the Mexican War Diedrick Dutchover lived in San Antonio for a time. He gained experience as a frontier scout and in 1850 the famous frontiersman "Big Foot" Wallace asked him to serve as shotgun on the first stage run from San Antonio to El Paso. He continued working for the stage line and married Refugia Salcedo. When not serving as a guard, he operated a small sheep ranch in Limpia Canyon. Later he acquired cattle. After the U.S. Army established Fort Davis in 1854, he sold milk to the post.

Indian attacks were a constant threat. When the 8th Infantry left in 1861, Dutchover took refuge in the fort to await the expected Confederate troops during the American Civil War. There were not enough soldiers to man the post permanently. So, when the Confederates evacuated, they left Dutchover in charge. Soon after the troops departed, Chief Nicolas and 250 Apaches swooped down on Fort Davis. Dutchover, with his family and four Americans, had no time to escape. They hid on a rooftop. After forty-eight hours the Indians grew tired of looting and began to scatter. One of the Americans on the rooftop was dying and could not be moved. So, on the third night he was left in hiding. Dutchover led the others toward Presidio, ninety-two miles away. Four days later the exhausted party reached safety.

When U.S. troops returned in 1867, Dutchover served as an army contractor to haul timber from Sawmill Canyon for use in rebuilding the fort. Even with a heavy guard he would frequently lose oxen at night to the Apaches. Dutchover spent the rest of his days near Fort Davis and was still there when the last soldiers left in 1891. The Dutchover name remains prominent in far West Texas, where numerous descendants live today.[19]

Before Anton Diedrick arrived in Texas, several other Belgians had preceded him. Priests from Belgium served on France's ill-fated LaSalle expedition in 1684. Juan Banul became a master blacksmith

Diedrick Dutchover and his family. Institute of Texan Cultures illustration no. 74-1235

at the presidio of San Antonio during the 1720s. He helped build several of the Texas missions. In the 1840s Peter Shiner, a native of Luxembourg, settled in Victoria, Texas, where he became a successful merchant, land speculator, and stock raiser. In 1858 Peter delivered thirteen hundred horses purchased in Mexico to an Illinois buyer. His son Henry kept up the business and began buying land in western Lavaca County where he donated land for the town of Shiner, located fourteen miles west of Hallettsville. A few other Belgians immigrated to Galveston, Houston, and the area along the Rio Grande. However, only eight Belgians lived in the state in 1850—seven of them in San Antonio.

It was not until the 1880s that more Belgians came to Texas, still numbering less than three hundred foreign-born by the end of the century. Most of the Belgian immigrants came from the area of Ghent and were Roman Catholics who wanted to own their own land or business. The land was suitable to the Belgian style of intensive farming so they chose to live near San Antonio, where the only Belgian community formed. There, some worked as bakers, candle and soap makers, restaurant owners, or musicians. Most, however, wanted to farm. They became vegetable farmers, introducing cauliflower and kohlrabi to South Texas. Their small community based on a common geographic origin, a common Roman Catholic faith, and close family ties continued to receive a small number of Belgian immigrants until the start of World War I.

Few of the Belgian Texan farmers had enough money to buy land when they arrived, so they rented it. Insects and crop diseases as well as lack of water for crops caused problems. Water had to be purchased from those living along San Pedro Creek and hauled by wagons to the fields. To solve the water problem, Adolph Baeten and Herman Van Daele, two of the most successful Belgian Texan farmers, drilled one of the first artesian wells in the San Antonio area. This led to a unique system for irrigating crops. Rather than employ the system in which the water entered the field at oblique angles, the Belgians used a technique whereby the water entered at right angles. For example, they would divide a field into separate plots. Water from

the wells could then be directed to any of the plots. Once there, the water flowed simultaneously down the rows of the plot.

The irrigation techniques and hard work allowed the San Antonio Belgian vegetable farmers to profit and acquire their own farming lands. They eventually banded together to form the Bexar County Truck Growers Association to market their crops. The association urged members to grow vegetables year-round to provide a more stable market for their produce.

Once established, the Belgian Texans began to hold social get-togethers and practice pastimes such as they had back home. One form of entertainment involved *bolls,* a game they introduced to Texas. It is similar to shuffleboard. Men played it with bolls made of wood. The bolls, or disks, looked like flat cheeses. The idea was to

Prosper Vervaet and Aviel Bauwens with their families and a wagon load of vegetables ready to take to market in San Antonio, ca. 1908. Institute of Texan Cultures illustration no. 68-3183

Belgian families introduced the game of bolls *to Texas, ca. 1935.* Institute of Texan Cultures illustration no. 75-695

roll the boll in an arc to land close to a peg at the end of a runway. A person won if his boll was closest to the peg and not hit away by an opponent. Women participated in the game by rolling the boll into a small box rather than hitting a peg.

The Belgian Texans also introduced in San Antonio the celebration known as Kermess, a fall festival held on August 15 and November 17, if there was a good crop.[20] Good harvests meant lots of fresh vegetables from the fields. One of the traditional favorites was Belgian red cabbage.

Belgian Red Cabbage
1 small head red cabbage
¼ cup vinegar
1 apple, cored and sliced
2 teaspoons sugar

1 diced onion
salt and pepper to taste
¼ cup red wine
1 tablespoon butter or margarine
1 bay leaf

Shred cabbage finely. Add all other ingredients. Stew in a heavy saucepan until cabbage is tender, about 1 hour. Add small amount of water or more wine to keep from burning. Keep pan covered. Cook over slow heat. Remove bay leaf before serving.

Another favorite food of the Belgian Texans is raisin bread. Mrs. John Waddell of San Antonio, who provided her mother's recipe from the early 1900s, recalls, "On Saturdays my mom would bake all day. She loved to cook for all the nieces and nephews. One pumpkin would make eighteen to twenty pies and we would each get a pie for ourselves. I have seven brothers and it thrills me when I use Mom's recipes and they say, 'Boy, this is just like Mamma made.'"

Belgian Raisin Bread
4 cups flour
¼ cup sugar
1 package active dry yeast
½ cup water
1 teaspoon salt
½ cup raisins
½ cup milk
2 eggs, slightly beaten
½ cup butter or margarine

Mix two cups flour with yeast. Stir water, milk, butter, sugar, and salt over low heat until the butter melts and add to the yeast mixture. Add remaining flour, raisins, and eggs. Knead until dough is smooth and elastic. Grease two 1-pound coffee cans. Divide the dough in half and place in cans. Cover with plastic tops. Let rise until dough reaches 1" from the top. Bake at 375° for 35 minutes.

THE SWISS TEXANS

1870: 599
1890: 1,711
1900: 1,709
1910: 1,773

Cheese often reminds people of Switzerland. In the 1850s Johann U. Anderegg brought the art of cheese making to the Texas Hill Country. His father, a prosperous Swiss lawyer, had allowed Johann to travel throughout Europe, where he learned to speak German, Italian, and English.

In his early 30s, Johann decided to settle in Texas. He chose a homesite on Beaver Creek between Fredericksburg and Mason. His house was of rock and timber, two stories high. The ground floor was divided into two rooms, while upstairs was a large single open area. A part of this dwelling was a cubicle from which the home could be defended against Indian attack. With the heavy door bolted, gunfire could be directed from a series of narrow loopholes in the wall. Sixty yards from the house was a spring over which Anderegg built a rock structure that served as a cooling room. Inside, flat stones were arranged to form walkways, around which water flowed. Above these walks were shelves on which cheeses and other foods were kept. The thick walls and cool spring water created an ideal environment for curing the cheeses for which Anderegg became locally famous. His cheeses were shaped into large discs 2½' in diameter, 5" thick, and weighed nearly 50 pounds.[21]

Johann Anderegg was typical of the Swiss who came to Texas during the 1800s. The Swiss were an educated people, and many were of German, French, or Italian origin. They were usually Protestants or Roman Catholics. The population was very democratic and prosperous. As a result, few Swiss decided to leave their homeland. Those like Anderegg who came to Texas did so seeking new adventures or to avoid the required military service. They immigrated mainly as individuals and seldom came in groups.

While never many in total numbers when compared with the Germans, English, or Irish (only 599 Swiss by 1870), Swiss Texans nonetheless contributed to the development of Texas and quickly joined the mainstream. Charles Amsler, for example, fought in the 1835 siege of Bexar during the Texas Revolution. John Hermann arrived in Houston during 1838. Using the proceeds from the sale of his wife's jewelry, Hermann and his family opened one of that city's

Swissman Alex Schneider, Sr., with the first brass band in the Grey County town of Pampa. Institute of Texan Cultures illustration no. 76-60

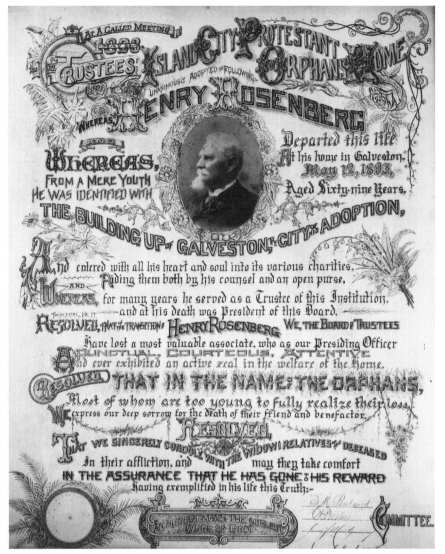

Legal resolution creating the Island City Orphans Home at the death of Henry Rosenberg in 1893. Institute of Texan Cultures illustration no. 68-2695

first dairies. George, their son, became successful in real estate. At his death, he left funds for building a hospital and land for what is now Hermann Park.

Henry Rosenberg settled in Galveston during 1843 and became successful in the mercantile, banking, and railroad businesses. When he died in 1893, he provided in his will funds to build an Episcopal church, the Galveston Orphans Home, and the famous Rosenberg Library.

In 1855, twenty-five Swiss settled in France's La Réunion colony near Dallas. Being academics or artisans, they were unable to make a living off the land and most moved to Dallas. Beginning in the 1880s Chris Streit and John Hirshi helped to further the cattle-ranching industry in North Texas. Cesar Maurice Lombardi arrived in Texas during 1871 and entered the newspaper business. By the early 1900s he was president of the A. H. Belo Corporation, which owned the *Galveston News,* the *Dallas Morning News,* and the *Dallas Evening Journal.* Also in Dallas, Jacob Metzger founded the dairy company that bore his name. Peter H. Mansbendel, a master woodcarver in the old Swiss tradition, made his home in Austin. One Texan of Swiss descent even served as president of the United States. He was born Dwight David Eisenhower in Denison, Texas, on October 14, 1890. His mother was a descendant of German Swiss who arrived in America before 1776.[22]

The peak in the Swiss population occurred between 1890 and 1920 when there were Swiss settlements in Bexar, Dallas, Austin, Fayette, Travis, and Williamson Counties. The Swiss also settled the town of Vernon, fifty miles northwest of Wichita Falls in the northern part of Wilbarger County, in 1893.

The Swiss who immigrated to Texas during the nineteenth century quickly disappeared into the general population. In fact, so well did they and their children become "Americanized" that there is little evidence of their Swiss culture. A few Swiss Texan women still on special occasions perform a traditional dance in their snowy outer garment called a chemise or chemisette, a peasant outfit worn throughout their native homeland. The chemise has lace-edged cuffs to match ruffling around the neck. The main cotton garment has a deep blue bodice that flares into a bright red peplum or ruffle laced with scarlet ties. Worn with this is a waltz-length blue skirt flared with a scarlet silk apron tied over it. All this is worn with a black scarf folded into a triangle and worn around the neck.[23]

Playing the alpenhorn, a ten-foot pipelike instrument that sounds like the deep bellow of a cow, is another fine example of the Swiss dedication to their cultural heritage. Swiss men once used it to signal one another across the mountains or to call their cattle. This unusual musical instrument remains a rich legacy of the Swiss.

Some Swiss Texans celebrate August 1, their homeland's national holiday. On that day in 1291, Switzerland became an independent nation when four farming communities united together as one country for protection from large landowners who desired to expand their kingdoms. To celebrate, the 32,304 (1990)[24] Texans of Swiss descent may choose to dine on a favorite veal entrée.

Emmenthal Veal Schnitzel
4 veal cutlets, well pounded
flour
1 egg, beaten
lemon juice
bread crumbs
salt and pepper
4–5 tablespoons butter
1 teaspoon grated cheese
4 slices Gruyere cheese, same size as cutlets

Sprinkle cutlets with lemon juice, salt, pepper, and a little cheese. Leave for 5 minutes, then roll in flour, beaten egg, and bread crumbs. Fry on one side in hot butter. Turn, reduce heat, place a slice of Gruyere cheese on the fried side of each cutlet, and fry the other side very slowly. Serve with crisp salad. Makes 4 servings.

The Swiss are also known for their fine desserts such as walnut pie.

Swiss Walnut Pie
Filling:
1½ cups sugar
2 cups walnuts, chopped
2 tablespoons honey
½ cup light cream

Crust:
2¼ cups sifted flour
¼ teaspoon salt
¼ cup butter
⅓ cup sugar
1 egg, beaten
1 tablespoon water

Melt sugar in a large skillet over medium heat. Stir constantly until a golden syrup is formed. Add walnuts and honey, stirring well. Then stir in the light cream and allow to cool.

Crust: Combine flour and salt in a medium bowl. Cut in butter until mixture is like cornmeal. Add ⅓ cup sugar, egg, and water and mix well. Form into a smooth ball. Wrap dough in wax paper and refrigerate until well chilled. Keep about half of the dough for later use. On a lightly floured surface, roll the remaining dough into a circle ¼" thick. Fold in half, place in a 9" pie pan, unfold, and press to fit the pan. Trim even with the top edge. Spread walnut mixture over dough in pan and fold sides of dough down over filling. Roll out remaining dough into a 9" circle. Place on filling and press edges together with a floured fork. Bake at 350° for 50 minutes or until top is golden. Cool on a wire rack and refrigerate until time to serve. Can be served topped with ice cream or whipped cream if desired.

CHAPTER 2
Northern Europe

THE DANISH TEXANS

1870: 159
1890: 649
1900: 1,089
1910: 1,289

"We are the sons of Vikings!" This was the cry of hardworking Danes making a new home in Texas. Ove Nielsen, a fellow countryman, expressed a similar attitude in his early-twentieth-century poem:

> *Gone is the Viking who battled the wave*
> *But never his spirit will rest in the grave.*
> *We are Americans, fruit of the Danes,*
> *The blood of the Viking is warm in our veins.*[1]

Though few in number compared to other European immigrant groups who came to Texas, the Danes nonetheless contributed greatly to the state's history. The first Danes to arrive in Texas were sailors like Peter Johnson who sailed his own ships along the Texas coast in 1832. Charles Zanco was not a sailor but an artist who died defending the Alamo in 1836. Before his death, he painted a single star on blue silk, thus creating the "Independence Flag" of the Lynchburg Company. The flag was carried at the battle of Concepción and the siege of Bexar during the fall of 1835.

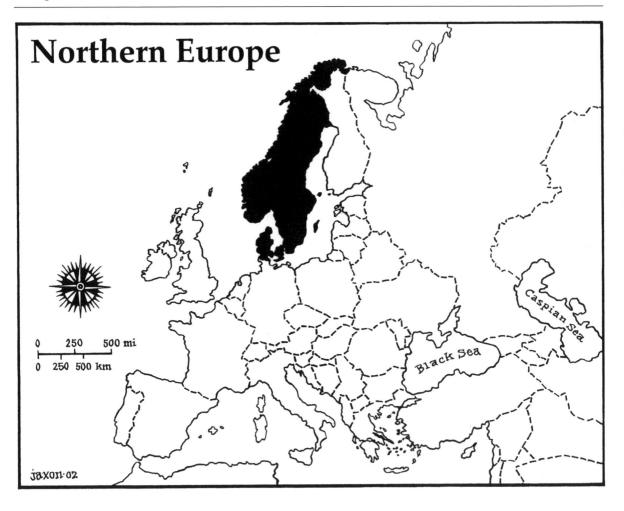

Northern Europe

jaxon·02

Northern Europe. Map by
Jack Jackson

By 1850 a few more Danes began to arrive. Hans Peter Nielsen Gammel, who came to America in 1874, was another Danish contributor to Texas history. After trying his luck in a futile effort to find gold, he settled in Austin and sent for his family in Denmark. Gammel opened up a business selling books. In 1881 a fire destroyed the state capitol building, and Gammel got the job of salvaging the state's records. He published this material in ten volumes called *Laws of Texas 1822–1897*. In the process he became the state printer while keeping his bookstore business.[2]

Other individual Danes came to Texas and settled throughout the state during the early to mid-1800s, but as organized groups the

▼▼▼

Danes did not begin to arrive until the late 1870s. It was then that two Texans, Travis Shaw and John Hester, visited Denmark and began to recruit new settlers to north-central Texas. The area became part of present-day Lee County, and some twenty Danish families settled near Lexington, sixteen miles north of Giddings. More Danish men, mostly farmers, followed and later sent for their families. As one Danish Texan said, "I did not want to be a common laborer in my own country."

The most successful effort to settle Danes in Texas occurred at Danevang, meaning Danish Field, in the southern part of Wharton County, eleven miles south of El Campo, in 1894. Sponsored by the Dansk Folkesamfund, the Danish People's Society, several hundred Danes who had first settled in the American Midwest arrived and began to acquire land. Their goal was to create a place in America that preserved Danish culture. Sponsoring the adventure was the

The Ansgar Lutheran Church in Danevang, ca. 1908. Institute of Texan Cultures illustration no. 78-348

Two Danish women hoeing cotton on the Peterson farm near Danevang. Institute of Texan Cultures illustration no. 72-742

Danish Evangelical Lutheran Church, whose members were called "Happy Danes." These Danes did not want to assimilate but wanted to maintain and preserve their distinct Danish culture. This distinguished them from the United Danish Lutheran Church, whose members became known as "Holy Danes" or "Gloomy Danes," a much sterner group who favored assimilation into the American culture.

The Danes at Danevang first tried to raise cold-weather grains, as they had in Denmark, but the grain crops did poorly in the Gulf Coast soil. Additionally, the cattle they brought with them contracted local diseases and most died. Moreover, having to deal with fields often too wet to plough made life miserable for the new settlers. The first year they lived on a diet of chickens, deer, berries, and sweet potatoes. Their crop failures also meant they could not meet the first payment on the loan they had taken to buy the land. When that occurred, Herman Kuntz, president of the Texas Land and Cattle

Company, helped them. The hard work of the Danevang Danes so impressed him that he got them an extension on the loan, which they soon paid off.

By the early twentieth century, the Danevang Danes had switched successfully to growing cotton and raising local cattle. One of the settlers, Margrethe Henningsen, recalled her mother's experience trying to milk a "Texan" cow. "We looked askance at the new cow, for it was a real Texas cow with long horns out to the sides. But it proved to be quite gentle as long as there was enough cottonseed in the feedbag. It was just a matter of getting through first. If the cow finished eating first, she ran, and then we either had to get more feed or content ourselves with what milk we had."[3]

As the Danevang residents began to prosper, they remained somewhat isolated from other Texans due to unpaved roads and the

Danes in Danevang shipping cottonseed at the train depot. Institute of Texan Cultures illustration no. 98-483

absence of telephones and electricity. Forced to rely on its own resources, the community started a cooperative economic system. The settlers helped one another in building homes and barns and created a farmers' cooperative to provide a better market for their goods. When times were hard, they could buy things together, "bulking," and get lower prices as well as sell their crops for better prices.

The Danes established their own public school where the children learned not only the standard subjects but also studied the history and language of the Danes. A common saying among many of the Danish Texans was "certainly we use English every day, but if we don't teach the children Danish, what will they do when they get to heaven?" However, by the twentieth century, English replaced Danish at Danevang church activities, and the children attended public school in El Campo where teachers taught only in English.

Despite their assimilation into Texan society, the Danevang Danes left behind some of their unique European customs and celebrations. Their Fall Festival lasted a week and began with a visiting pastor giving the Sunday service. Then he or other invited speakers, storytellers, or sometimes college professors, such as those in the field of agriculture, held afternoon and evening meetings through Friday. Saturday was the time for a daylong community picnic or fishing trip to the coast. The festivities concluded on Sunday with another church service.[4]

Other important celebrations involved twenty-fifth and fiftieth wedding anniversaries during which members of the community gave money to purchase a gift for the couple. Twenty-fifth anniversaries called for gifts made from silver such as silverware, trays, or bowls, while golden anniversaries meant the couple would receive items in gold such as gold watches. On the day of the anniversary, everyone gathered at the community hall for coffee—always coffee—and a variety of foods. The celebration also called for speakers to tell funny stories about the couple—all in good, clean fun. Some days later, the honored couple would host a dance at the community center or hold an open house at their home.

Birthdays were times for celebration as well.

▼▼▼

As a person's birthday approached, the women of his or her family began to bake. Though there was no single cake identified as the birthday cake, there were cakes, cookies, and pies to feed anyone and everyone who cared to drop by on the birthday afternoon to offer congratulations. There might be "six or six dozen" visitors; you never knew, since no invitations were given. The guests, forbidden by tradition to bring gifts or food, brought only themselves and their good wishes. Since no invitations were extended, everyone was automatically expected to be there.

There were also the twin Independence Day celebrations held every summer, a month apart, on June 5 and July 4. All day long on those two days, Danish Independence Day and American Independence Day, the whole community celebrated with games like sack races, turtle races, ring riding (in which a ring was caught from horseback or even "bicycle-back"), or dollar and horseshoe pitching. The Danish flag and the American flag flew side by side, "with maybe the

A group of Danish Texans take a day off to go swimming off the Gulf Coast. Institute of Texan Cultures illustration no. 98-566

▼▼▼

Young boys at Arthur Anderson's home near Danevang prepare for a bicycle race. Institute of Texan Cultures illustration no. 98-510

American flag a little higher." There were speeches and dancing to fiddle music and much high spirits far into the evenings.[5]

At these holiday gatherings, the women served dessert. A favorite was *aeblekage* (apple cake).

Danish Apple Cake (**Aeblekage**)
1½ pounds dried apples
¾ cup sugar
1 cup whipping cream
¼ cup melted butter
1 tablespoon sugar

▼▼▼

½ teaspoon vanilla
3 cups toasted white bread crumbs

Cook apples with ¾ cup sugar and water. Combine butter and crumbs in a skillet over low heat and mix well. Whip cream, adding 1 tablespoon sugar and vanilla. On a platter, place a thin layer of apples and then crumbs, alternating layers; cover with whipped cream. Makes about 12 servings.

Of course, no matter what the occasion or for none at all, the Danish Texans had the tradition of taking special breaks that meant eating pastries and drinking coffee at ten in the morning and three in the afternoon.

A Danish woman in her kitchen with a new stove. Institute of Texan Cultures illustration no. 98-415

▼▼▼

77

THE NORWEGIAN TEXANS

1870: 403
1890: 1,313
1900: 1,359
1910: 1,785

Elise Amalie Tvede Waerenskjold, who arrived in Texas during 1847, was a most unusual woman. This outspoken woman was born in Norway, February 19, 1815, the daughter of Norwegian Lutheran minister Nicolai Tvede and his wife, Johanne Elizabeth Tvede. They hired private tutors to educate Elise at home, and she became fluent not only in Norwegian but also in English, German, and French.

Elise was an independent thinker who wanted women to have the same rights as men. By age nineteen she began a teaching career—something few women then dared to do in Norway. Then she established her own private school for girls, again something women just did not do.

While still managing her school, Elise married Svend Foyn, a struggling young sea captain who later in life became wealthy after inventing the harpoon cannon used in modern whaling. The marriage was not destined to last though, especially since Svend wanted Elise to give up her teaching career and stay at home "to iron my shirts and darn my socks." Thus, after being wed for only three years, the couple had a friendly divorce. For her day and age, Elise again did something unusual for the 1840s. She discarded the surname of Svend Foyn's.

Even before marrying Svend, Elise had become an outspoken reformer. She spoke out for women's rights and opposed any form of slavery. She also published several articles condemning the abuses associated with excessive drinking of alcoholic beverages. Her articles impressed Johan R. Reiersen, co-owner of a monthly reform magazine called *Norway and America,* who was a supporter of Norwegian immigration to America. When Reiersen took a group of Norwegians to Texas, he made Elise editor of his magazine. At the time, few females anywhere in the world managed a magazine.

Elise and Wilhelm Waerenskjold and their children, Otto and Niels. Institute of Texan Cultures illustration no. 68-2591

At age thirty-two, Elise joined another group of Norwegians and came to Texas in 1847. On September 10, 1848, she married the leader of the expedition to Texas, Wilhelm Waerenskjold. The couple settled at Four Mile Prairie, bordering on Van Zandt and Kaufman Counties. They had a 1,250-acre farm where Elise gave birth to three sons, Otto, Niels, and Thorvald.

At Four Mile Prairie, the Waerenskjolds struggled to earn a living by farming and ranching their land. Elise continued to write letters about Texas to her friends in Norway. Norwegian newspapers and journals published many of her letters. One such letter, dated July 9, 1851, received wide circulation in her home country. In the letter she noted,

> You are acquainted with my views about immigration to this country. I believe now, as formerly, that there are many thousands in Norway who would be far happier over here, namely, the growing class of laborers . . . yes, also the less well-to-do farmers and handicraftsmen; in short, all people in Norway who live in economic dependence and have to work for others. Since the wages here are so much better, people like that could work themselves up in a short time to an independent position free of worries about daily bread. On the other hand, anyone who is well situated in Norway ought, in my opinion, to remain. . . . For the poor and destitute, on the other hand, who have never enjoyed things like these, but from early childhood have been inured to drudgery and toil, there is little to lose and much to gain. . . . Land can still be obtained in our neighborhood for $.35 to $2 per acre. Lots as small as 320 acres are still obtainable at $.50 per acre, but this will not last long, as land is rising in price. . . .
>
> A family with children will get ahead much easier than one without, since labor is of greater value than in Norway and many kinds of work can be done by children as well as by adults. . . . In New Orleans immigrants [coming to Texas] should provide themselves with quinine, castor oil, and other useful medicines. . . .[6]

Aside from writing letters to Norway encouraging others to move to Texas, Elise, to bring the family some added income, sold books, taught school, and took orders for magazines and garden seeds. Somehow the Waerenskjolds, like their Norwegian neighbors, managed to survive the hardships of living on what was then a frontier region in North Texas. Like most other Texans, they had to endure plagues of insects, poor crops due to the lack of rainfall, loss of livestock, financial hardship, and the threat of Indian attacks.

▼▼▼

Horrible tragedy struck the family twice during 1866. First, Thorvald, age seven and the youngest son of the Waerenskjolds, died. Next, for reasons unknown today, a Methodist preacher named N. T. Dickerson encountered Wilhelm at the Prairieville post office in Kaufman County and killed him. After stabbing Wilhelm, Dickerson fled. When brought to trial nine years later, he received a ten-year prison sentence for second-degree murder. Elise wrote that it was "a mild punishment to be sure, for such cold-blooded and long-premeditated murder."

However, not even the deaths of her son and husband deterred Elise. She continued to manage the farm and raise her two surviving sons. She never wavered in her belief in the essential equality of all men and women. Just after the Civil War ended, Elise wrote to a friend in Norway. In the letter she recalled how on more than one occasion and in violation of the law before and during the Civil War, she had not only spoken out against the institution of slavery but had fed and sheltered fugitive or runaway slaves.

Until the war I did not really know the laws on slavery; but I know now that according to these laws I was guilty of [criminal] offenses more than a hundred times, because the law decreed several years of penal servitude [or time served in prison] only for saying in a private conversation that slavery was unjust. The same punishment was stipulated for helping a fugitive slave in any way; for example, giving him a meal, a night's lodging, or similar aid. Now the slaves are finally free, but as yet their freedom does not mean very much because their former owners try to scare them into remaining, and many of them have actually been killed. Some, however, have left their masters, or the latter have voluntarily sent them on their way. But what of the thousands of people who have nothing with which to make a start in life—many even lacking the clothes they need to cover their bodies? For great numbers of them, life will be harsher now than when they were slaves. Practically all the Norwegians have hired Negroes, and among us they are well-treated. . . .[7]

▼▼▼

Elise lived to see her two surviving sons married with families of their own. In her later years, she took turns living with them. And, until her death at the age of eighty on January 22, 1895, at Hamilton, Texas, home of Otto, this early feminist and civil rights advocate continued to speak out about her belief in the basic dignity and equality of all people.

The Waerenskjold family was typical of the mostly rural Norwegians who moved to Texas. Most were Lutheran farmers seeking a life better than the working-class life they had in Norway. The articles and letters from the early immigrants to Texas and other states encouraged more than 260,000 Norwegians to come to America between 1879 and 1893.

Other Norwegians arrived in Texas even earlier than the Waerenskjolds. Johannes Nordboe at age seventy came with his family and settled on a plot of land in Dallas County during 1841. A few other families followed Nordboe, but it was not until 1845 that the first real Norwegian settlement got under way.

Johan Reinert Reiersen, considered the father of Norwegian immigration, along with his brother had a liberal newspaper in Norway promoting immigration. He arrived in America in 1843 to look at several possible places for a Norwegian settlement and decided to visit Texas. He met Republic of Texas President Sam Houston, who told him that Texas would welcome a Norwegian settlement. Reiersen returned to Norway where he and about ten others made plans to move to Texas. They started their settlement on land in northeastern Texas near present-day Brownsboro. When many of the settlers at Brownsboro died, Reiersen moved farther west and founded a second colony at Four Mile Prairie where the Waerenskjolds joined him. The Norwegians came in groups planning to start communities and maintained a lively correspondence with family and friends back home, many of whom decided to join them in Texas. The 1850 census listed 105 Norwegian-born persons living in Texas, but immigration continued until 1872 with the 1900 census listing 1,359 Norwegians.

The largest of the early Norwegian colonies in Texas was in

A self-portrait of Johannes Nordboe painted in 1792 at age twenty-four. Institute of Texan Cultures illustration no. 68-2540

Bosque County, northwest of Waco. In 1853 Cleng Peerson, Ole Canuteson, and Karl Questad persuaded a number of families to leave a Norwegian colony in Illinois and move there. The group created the Texas towns of Norse, Clifton, and Cranfills Gap. According to one account,

> [the] first homes in the Bosque settlements were built of logs or, occasionally, of stone. The ends of the logs were notched so that they could be crossed and fitted together at the corners. Caulking was necessary to fill cracks in the walls. Stone houses were much more difficult to build, since the stone had to be quarried and shaped by hand with hammers, chisels and saws.

The Waerenskjold residence at Four Mile Prairie surrounded by a split-rail fence. Institute of Texan Cultures illustration no. 68-2573

Early settlers in Bosque County held "fencing bees" to build stake fences. For days before, the men of the settlement cut and sharpened posts, which were then hauled to the field where the fence was to be constructed. They drove the posts into the ground and bound them together at the top with wire. Where the ground was not amenable to driving stakes, rock fences were built.[8]

No matter where Norwegian Texans lived, like the Waerenskjold family, they opposed slavery. The Norwegian hatred of slavery was evident in their hiring of free blacks at wages equal to whites to work for them. Two such free blacks, Frank and Patsy Bean, worked for the Swensen family in Norse during the Civil War. When the widow Swensen moved to Clifton in 1890, Frank and Patsy stayed in

Norse but continued to work for Mrs. Swensen and her children. Over the years Frank and Patsy had learned to speak Norwegian.

When more Norwegians began to move to the Bosque County area in the 1890s, Frank would meet the new arrivals as they got off the train. One story recounts that "Frank greeted them with smiles and in perfect Norwegian asked solicitous question as to their

Five-year-old Sadie Swanson Hoel holds her doll. Institute of Texan Cultures illustration no. 71-439

welfare and wishes. Having hardly even seen a black before, they were naturally thunderstruck. . . . Frank's ebony color startled them. And they were hardly comforted in the scorching Texas sun when Frank deadpanned, 'I wouldn't worry; things will be all right. When you have been here in this hot sun as long as I, you may be black, too.'"⁹

Central to the life at Norse was Our Savior's Lutheran Church, established in 1869.

> The business of the church was entirely in the hands of the men. The offering was given once a month when the members marched around the altar, laying their money on the altar. It was the custom for the women and children to sit on one side of the aisle, and the men on the other, during services.
>
> After Sunday services, there was much visiting in the homes. Hospitality was extended to all, especially to those coming from a distance. . . .

Wedding ceremonies also served as social events with all the neighbors joining in the joyous time.

> The ceremony was performed at twelve o'clock noon. Immediately after it concluded, the friends and kinsmen joined the wedding party in marching back to the home of the bride, where the reception was held. It was an old-time reception, many days having been used to prepare four kinds of cake, several kinds of cookies, and a large wedding cake, which had been decorated with large and small candy hearts. This was in addition to one hog and one calf, which had been made up into different cuts of meats. . . .
>
> It was the tradition that the feast was followed with dancing to the accompaniment of stringed instruments. If no instruments were available, a caller would still call the dancers to swing or square dance or do Norwegian folk dances. When musicians were available the waltz, the polka, and the schottische were favorite dances. . . .
>
> Dancing became an art with the Norwegian pioneers. Shoes were hard to get; consequently, if the distance wasn't too great, the dancers

would carry their shoes as they walked to the party, putting them on just before reaching the home of the hosts.[10]

Many such Norwegian Texan customs have gone out of practice; however, descendants continue to serve traditional foods of Norway. One of the best known includes the cooking of stockfish, which is cod. The stockfish serves as the basis of a lutefisk dinner. In Norwegian, lutefisk comes from the word *lute,* which means to wash in a lye solution, and *fisk,* meaning fish. It applies to cod, haddock, or hake that is dried in the open air without using salt. The fish is soaked in limewater and then cleaned by soaking in clear water for ninety-six hours. Next, it is boiled in cheesecloth bags before serving. Not many non-Norwegians seem to like lutefisk.

Mrs. Christine Dahl was the only woman allowed to vote in the Norse Lutheran Church because she was a widow. Institute of Texan Cultures illustration no. 73-1753

Other traditional favorites still enjoyed by the 94,096 (1990)[11] Texans of Norwegian descent include the following:

Norwegian Split-Pea Soup
1 pound of ham hock
dash of red pepper
1 large onion
1 pound dry split peas
salt and pepper to taste
2 bay leaves

Cut up ham hock and put into a kettle with peas, bay leaves, onion, and 2 quarts of water. Boil slowly for about 2 hours or until peas are completely done; add seasonings. Remove onion, ham hocks, and bay leaves. Makes 8 to 10 servings.

Norwegian Christmas Bread
1 cup butter
1 cup sugar
4 cups milk, scalded
2 yeast cakes
4 cups flour or more
½ teaspoon cardamom
½ cup chopped pecans
¾ cup raisins
¼ cup citron
½ cup candied cherries

Melt butter and sugar in milk; cool to lukewarm and add yeast. Add cardamom and flour. Knead well and let rise until light. Add fruit and nuts and knead again. Shape into loaves in a loaf pan, let rise, and bake at 350° for 1 hour. Frost with a cream made of powdered sugar and milk. Cool completely before serving. Makes two loaves.

THE SWEDISH TEXANS

1870: 364
1890: 2,896
1900: 4,388
1910: 4,706

Pehr Andersson Sjoholm at age eighteen followed in the footsteps of his father. In 1846 he became a cavalryman in the Swedish army. Six years later he married Catherina Olsson, another Swedish native. The Sjoholms would have nine children—eight of whom lived well into adulthood.

Like other Swedes, the Sjoholms were literate in their native language. The Swedish Evangelical Lutheran Church, the official church of Sweden, required all of its citizens to be able to read anything needed for church services. Even those who were not members of the church were expected to become literate.

Most of the Sjoholm family was destined to immigrate to the United States. In 1881 Pehr Sjoholm resigned from the army in order to seek a better-paying occupation and decided to embark on a new life in America. One of his sons, Carl Emanuel, also a former member of the Swedish Cavalry, who lived in Hartford, Connecticut, had obtained U.S. citizenship and had married Swede Christina Swenson. Pehr and two of his other sons, Axel, who likewise had served in the Swedish Cavalry, and Julius, boarded the *City of Berlin* and sailed from Liverpool, England, to New York. They traveled to Rockford, Illinois, where Sophie, Pehr and Catherina's daughter, and her Swedish husband, Swen Martin, had immigrated. The Sjoholms stayed there for two years until Catherina and another daughter, Amanda, joined them. Gustaf, another son, saved enough money for passage to America and went to Bridgeport, Connecticut, where he soon married Swede Emma Persdotter. A last son, Oalf, had married in Sweden and remained there.

Texas enticed all of the Sjoholms but Olaf to make a move. In 1887 Pehr and Catherina decided to move to New Sweden in Travis

County. There Axel and his wife, Anna Katrina, joined them. Son Julius lived close by in Austin where he made his living as a stonecutter.

In New Sweden, Pehr and Catherina became charter members of the Swedish Bethlehem Lutheran Church in nearby Lund. Pehr probably named the community—a name taken from "the beautiful City of Lund located near his boyhood home in Sweden."

Pehr, Axel, and Gustaf worked first as carpenters in Lund. Soon they rented land for cotton and corn farming. Gustaf also worked as a co-owner of the local general store. All three applied for U.S. citizenship, and in the process Gustaf changed the spelling of his surname to "Seaholm," a name which subsequent generations of the family continued. Pehr Anglicized his first name to "Peter" but still signed his name as "Pehr." Gustaf and Pehr became American citizens in 1892. Axel never completed the citizenship process.

Ernest, one of Pehr and Catherina's grandsons, recalled that his grandfather was a large man who could be rather gruff. No matter—he did everything Catherina, a small woman, told him to do. Both Pehr and Catherina spoke Swedish to their grandchildren so that the grandchildren could learn it while also acquiring English. Ernest recalled the death of his mother, Axel's wife, in 1885. Pehr drove a wagon pulled by two mules that took Anna Katrina in her coffin to be buried in the New Sweden cemetery.

Most of the Seaholms continued to live in the Lund area and were later joined by Annette, Pehr and Catherina's other daughter, and her Swedish husband as well as by the Carl Emanuel family. Carl Emanuel, who had gone to Hartford in 1879 following his departure from the Swedish army, became a harness maker there. When he saw the first mechanical car on the streets of Hartford, he knew his days as a harness maker were numbered. That made him decide to move to Texas. All the family members in the Lund area eventually became successful landowning farmers.

Axel's second marriage was to another Swede, Selma Justina Andersdotter. Selma came to Texas at age twelve to live with a cousin. Originally, her family had bought a boat ticket for her older sister to

Pehr Andersson Sjoholm with sword and fencing medal. Courtesy of Ernest Mae Seaholm, Eagle Lake, Texas. Institute of Texan Cultures illustration no. 102-64

immigrate to America. When the older sister suddenly died, the family, not wanting to waste the money paid for the ticket, sent young Selma instead. Axel and Selma moved to Colorado County, Texas, in 1896. There he and the four sons by his first marriage, Gustaf, Ernest, Carl, and Helmer, became successful rice farmers and civic leaders of the community.

Typical of the many second and third generations of Swedish immigrant families to Texas, the four sons of Axel married non-Swedes. Also characteristic of many second and third generation Swedish Texans was that their children no longer learned the language of their ancestral homeland.[12]

The work of the earlier Swedish immigrants such as Swante Magnus Swenson made adjustment to Texas easier for the Seaholm family that followed. In Sweden, Swenson had worked as a bookkeeper, but tired of such an existence, he came to America at age 20, eventually arriving in Galveston, Texas, during 1838. He entered the mercantile business with a man in Columbus, Texas. Swenson went on to own a large plantation in Fort Bend County, a mercantile store and hotel business in Austin, the SMS Ranch, and held land certificates in a railroad.

Swenson's uncle, Swante Palm, joined Swenson in 1844 and became a business partner and later a civic leader in Austin. In 1897 Palm donated his twelve-thousand-volume library to the University of Texas at Austin, which increased the university library's holdings by 60 percent.

Swenson and Palm encouraged other Swedes to come to Texas. Their first effort, in 1848, brought twenty-five families, mostly relatives. Swenson helped these families and later others by loaning them the money for the ocean passage to Texas. He employed many of them, which allowed them to repay him. He also sold them land at a good price to start their own businesses.

Between 1869 and 1893 more than seven hundred thousand Swedes came to America, and they were the largest group of Scandinavians to come to Texas. They established themselves mainly in the Travis and Williamson Counties areas and gave Texas such place

▼▼▼

names as Govalle, Lund, Manda, New Sweden, Hutto, Swedonia, East Sweden, West Sweden, Palm Valley, Swensondale, and Bergstrom Air Force Base. Like the Seaholms, the early Swedes farmed in the rural areas of Texas where they "helped one another '*i filen*,' in the field with corn, wheat, oats, sugar cane, rice, and, most important, cotton. Girls milked the cows, made cheese and butter, and sold dairy products to augment farm income. Pigs were slaughtered in the fall and before Christmas. The meat was then either salted or smoked over oak bark, so that it would be preserved until summer. Many families joined *kottkulbbar* or meat clubs, in which they butchered animals weekly in a certain order, each family receiving particular portions in a rotating cycle."[13]

Other Texas Swedes entered into various businesses or teaching. One, geologist John Udden, did the mineral survey of university lands in West Texas in 1904. His survey helped provide for oil

Helmer, Gustaf, Carl, Ernest, and cousin Ed, five of Pehr and Catherina Sjoholm's (Seaholm's) grandsons atop their favorite horses at Eagle Lake. Courtesy of Ernest Mae Seaholm, Eagle Lake, Texas. Institute of Texan Cultures illustration no. 102-65

Swante "Swen" Magnus Swenson (1816–96) and wife, Jeanette Long. Institute of Texan Cultures illustration no. 68-2642

and natural gas explorations that made the University of Texas at Austin wealthy. Gustaf Belfrage of Norse, Texas, was a well-known naturalist who discovered 243 new species of insects. Another Swedish Texan, John Peter Sjolander of Cedar Bayou, became a well-known poet. One of his poems entitled "The Blue Bonnet of Texas" became a favorite frequently found in Texas schoolbooks.

> *It blooms upon our prairies wide*
> *And smiles within our valleys,*
> *A Texas flower and Texas pride,—*
> *Around it honor rallies;*
> *And every heart beneath the blue*
> *Transparent sky above it,*
> *In Texan-wise, forever true,*
> *Shall fold and hold and love it. . . .*[14]

The Texas Swedes represented various religious groups. About 60 percent were members of the Swedish Lutheran Church. Some 37 percent were members of the Swedish Methodist Episcopal Church. Others were either members of the Baptists or the Swedish Evangelical Free Church. Those in the latter group emphasized the personal experience of grace and interpreted the Bible literally. Their congregations avoided church organizations that had districts, conferences, or synods, which they considered a hindrance to true worship. Instead, they focused their efforts on mission work.

Some of the religious groups established their own institutions of higher learning such as the Swedish Trinity Lutheran College in Round Rock. Another was the Swedish Methodist Texas Wesleyan College in Austin. Both later closed for financial reasons.

Christmas represented a special time among Swedish Texans. The custom of honoring *jultomten,* the Swedish version of Father Christmas, the "Christmas elf," probably entered Texas with Swedish immigrants brought in by Swenson during 1848.

Ranch hands gather at the chuck wagon on the SMS Ranch in Jones County, Texas, ca. 1920. Institute of Texan Cultures illustration no. 90-3

Swedish residents of Travis and Williamson Counties swimming in a stream, ca. 1920. Institute of Texan Cultures illustration no. 90-288

At the time, *jultomten,* or *nissen,* was a tiny old man with a long white beard who lived in or around every peasant family's barn. To keep him happy (and to avoid such disasters as spoiled or spilt milk or open barn doors and wandering of livestock—all potentially his doing), one placated the little gnome with a dish of porridge *(julgrot)* every Christmas Eve. Nowadays he has had to shoulder greater responsibility, such as distributing presents to children, and has consequently greatly increased in size, so that he does resemble Santa Claus or Father Christmas....

Julotta is the Swedish early morning worship service on Christmas Day, in which the church is lit only by candlelight.... In addition to the use of lighted candles, a Swedish sermon was (and is) preached, and the best-loved Swedish Christmas hymns were sung. Chief among these in popularity were *"Var halsad skona morgonstund"* (Greetings Lovely Morning Hour), *"Stilla natt"* (Silent Night), and *"Betlehemsstjernan"* (the Star of Bethlehem)....

Christmas in Swedish Texas also meant traditional Swedish foods. The great Christmas ham *(julskinka)*, brown beans *(bruna bonor)*, and rice pudding *(rissgrynsgrot)* were served alongside American specialties such as sweet potatoes, tomatoes, and turkey. In many homes a cedar tree replaced the Swedish fir tree *(julgran)*, but the evening reading of the nativity story in Swedish by the head of the family remained the same as in the homeland, as did the custom of celebrating on Christmas Eve instead of the more American tradition of Christmas Day.[15]

Swedish women doing needlework outside the Ellen and John Holmberg residence in New Sweden, Texas, ca. 1910. Institute of Texan Cultures illustration no. 90-283

▼▼▼

Aside from their usual preferences for salted herring and cheese-cake, Swedish Texans had other traditional food specialties. Some of those enjoyed by the more than 155,193 (1990)[16] Texans of Swedish descent include the following:

Swedish Lutefish (Dried Cod)

Saw lutefish in 5" lengths and soak in water for two days. Drain. Make a solution of 1 heaping tablespoon lye and ⅓ cup slaked lime to each gallon of water used. Use a large stone or crock jar. Dissolve lye and lime in water in crock and place fish in the solution. Leave four days, stirring occasionally with a wooden paddle. After four days take fish out of solution and place in clear water for four days, changing the water each day. Keep well iced throughout the procedure.

To cook: Place the fish in an enameled vessel in enough salted water to cover well. When the water comes to a boil, watch closely, checking the fish with a fork. Cook until flaky, about 4 to 5 minutes. Do not overcook. Drain immediately. Serve with white sauce.

Swedish Potato Sausage (Potatis Korv)

2½ pounds ground pork butt
1 pound lean ground beef
6 potatoes, peeled and ground
1 medium onion, ground
1 tablespoon of sugar
1 cup milk, scalded and cooled
2 or 3 tablespoons of salt
1 teaspoon fresh ground pepper
¾ teaspoon fresh ground or crushed allspice
2 teaspoons ginger
1 pound casings

Mix meats and ground potatoes. Add milk and seasonings and mix thoroughly. Rinse salt off casings and soak in lukewarm water. Cut casings into desired lengths. Stuff using a sausage stuffer. Fill to about 1½ inches from end. It is not necessary to tie casings. Sausage is best if immersed in salt brine in the refrigerator for a couple of days. Before cooking, use a large needle to prick holes in the casings. While cooking, prick any bubbles that form in casings. Cook in boiler with enough water to cover. Simmer slowly for 1½ hours. This sausage may be frozen and reheated after initial cooking.

CHAPTER 3
Eastern Europe

THE GERMAN TEXANS

1870: 23,985
1890: 48,843
1900: 48,295
1910: 44,929

Germans comprised the largest European immigrant group in Texas. During the 1850s more than 1,000,000 Germans came to the United States with another 1,500,000 coming during the 1880s. Many of those came to Texas as farmers, craftsmen, and unskilled laborers hoping to improve their lives. The 1990 United States census revealed that 1,175,888 Texans claimed pure and 1,775,838 partial German ancestry, for a total of 2,951,726, or 17.5 percent of the total Texas population.[1]

German settlers clustered in small communities from Galveston and Houston westward to Kerrville in the Hill Country, forming what is known as the German Belt. Johann Friedrich Ernst was the first German to bring his family to Texas. In 1819 the Duke of Oldenburg, Germany, appointed him post office clerk, but ten years later he and his family fled the country. The Duke of Oldenburg charged him with embezzling a large amount of post office money. Ernst had planned to move his family to a German settlement in Missouri, but while in New Orleans on his way to Missouri, he learned that Texas offered better opportunities. Thus, in 1831, he

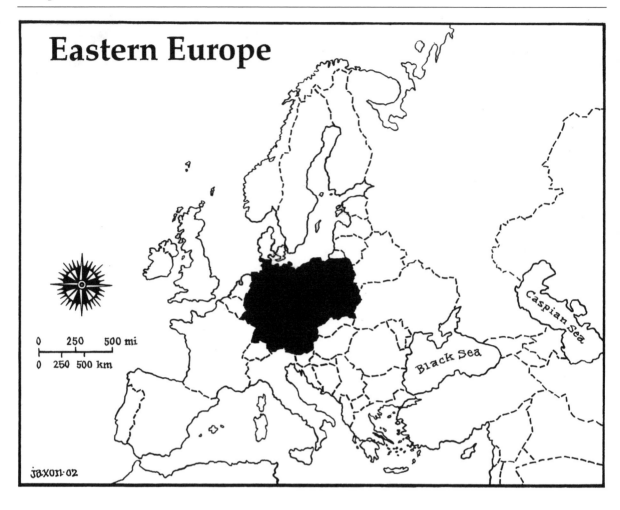

Eastern Europe

Eastern Europe. Map by
Jack Jackson

obtained a 4,428-acre land grant in Stephen F. Austin's colony. As an owner of a land grant, he had to improve it within two years, but he did not have to pay any taxes for at least six years. The owner was also supposed to be a Roman Catholic, but the Mexican government never enforced that rule.

So enthusiastic did Ernst become about Texas that on February 1, 1832, he wrote about this new land to a friend in Oldenburg. The friend had Ernst's letter published for other Germans to read. As a result, more Germans became interested in moving to Texas. People who were interested found it difficult to acquire land in Germany where land prices were too high for most to buy.

▼▼▼

Ernst had not really had time to know much about Texas other than his own local area, but in his letter he wrote,

Each immigrant who wishes to engage in farming receives a league of land; a single person, one quarter of a league. A league of land contains . . . mountain and valley, woods and meadows, cut through by brooks.

The ground is hilly and alternates with forest and natural grass plains. Various kinds of trees. Climate like that of Sicily. The soil needs no fertilizer. Almost constant east wind. No winter, almost like March in Germany. Bees, birds, and butterflies the whole winter through. A cow with a calf costs ten dollars. Planters who have seven hundred head of cattle are common. Principal products: tobacco, rice, indigo grow wild. Sweet potatoes, melons of an especial goodness, watermelons, wheat, rye. Vegetables of all kinds. Peaches in great quantity grow wild in the woods. Mulberries, many kinds of walnuts, wild plums, persimmons sweet as honey. . . . Honey is found chiefly in hollow trees. Birds of all kinds, from pelicans to hummingbirds. Wild prey such as deer, bears, raccoons, wild turkeys, geese . . . in quantity. Free hunting and fishing. Wild horses and buffalo in hordes. . . .

English the ruling speech. Clothing and shoes very dear. . . . The more children, the better for . . . field labor. Scarcely three months work a year. No need for money, free exercise of religion. And the best markets for all products at the Mexican harbors. . . . We men satisfy ourselves with hunting and horse races.

On account of the yellow fever [malaria], one should arrive some weeks before the month of July or after the first of October. It is a good thing if one can speak English. . . .[2]

Ernst's daughter, Caroline, had a different impression of Texas when she arrived with her family in 1831. Fortunately, her view of Texas was not made known to the hundreds of Germans who followed the Ernst family to Texas.

When my father brought me to Texas, I was eleven. . . . We set sail for Texas [from New Orleans] in the ship *Saltillo.* As we were ready to start, a flatboat with a party of Kentuckians and their dogs was tied to our boat. The Kentuckians came on board, leaving their dogs behind on the flatboat [tied to the *Saltillo*].

We had almost as little comfort as the dogs. The boat was jammed with people and their bags. You could hardly find a place on the floor to lie down. We landed at Harrisburg [near Galveston Bay and now part of Houston] on the 3d of April 1831. At that time it was made up of about five or six log houses. . . .

[Our house in Industry was] roofed with straw and had six sides. These were made out of moss. The roof was by no means water-proof. We often held an umbrella over our bed when it rained at night. We suffered a great deal in the winter. My father had tried to build a chimney and fireplace out of logs and clay. But we were afraid to light a fire because of our straw roof. So we had to be cold.

Our shoes gave out, and we had to go barefoot in winter. We did not know how to make moccasins. We did not have enough clothes, either. We had no spinning wheel. Nor did we know how to spin and weave like the Americans. It was 28 miles to San Felipe de Austin and, besides, we had no money. When we could buy things, my first calico dress cost 50 cents a yard.

We really had more house and farm tools than our neighbors. But they knew better how to help themselves. We ate nothing but corn bread at first. Later, we began to raise cow peas. Afterwards, my father made a fine vegetable garden. We had no cooking stove. We baked our bread in the only pan we owned. Since the nearest mill was 30 miles off, the ripe corn was boiled until it was soft. Then it was scraped and baked.[3]

Several German immigrants, having read or heard about Ernst's letter, arrived in time to take part in the Texas Revolution. A number were with Ben Milam's troops in the battle at San Antonio during 1835. Robert Justus Kleberg of Cat Spring fought for the Texans there as well as at San Jacinto on April 21, 1836. He later became a successful rancher whose descendants today operate the King Ranch in South Texas.

Another German immigrant, Herman Ehrenberg, also fought with Milam. He was one of the few to escape the massacre of James Fannin's men at Goliad during the spring of 1836. George Washington Smyth signed the Texas Declaration of Independence. Jacob Darst died defending the Alamo on March 6, 1836. German immigrants George B. Erath, John Karner, Christian Wertzner, and Frederick Lemsky fought with Sam Houston at San Jacinto. So many Germans had come to Texas by 1847 that the legislature agreed to publish laws in German as well as in English.

Most of the German immigrants came from west central Germany. One factor increasing the number of German immigrants was the work of the Society for the Protection of German Immigrants in Texas. In 1842 a group of wealthy Germans organized the *Verein,* meaning society. The organization purchased property for German farmers wishing to own land in Texas. After being deceived into buying poor farmland more suited for ranching, the *Vereins'* chief agent became Prince Carl of Solms-Braunfels. In 1845 he directed the founding of the town of New Braunfels. A dozen years later one traveler described New Braunfels: "Half the men now residing in Neu-Braunfels and its vicinity, are probably agricultural laborers, or farmers . . . . The majority of [them] do not . . . own more than ten acres of land each." Along with farmers, New Braunfels had skilled workers, such as twenty carpenters, eight blacksmiths, seven wagon-makers, six shoemakers, five tailors, and four bakers. He added that "there are four grist-mills. . . . A weekly newspaper is published—the *Neu-Braunfels Zeitung.* . . . There are ten or twelve stores and small tradesmen's shops, two or three apothecaries, and as many physicians, lawyers, and clergymen." In New Braunfels and the other German towns, "there are five free schools for elementary education, one exclusive Roman Catholic school, a town free school of higher grade, and a private classical school. In all of these schools English is taught with German."[4]

John O. Meusebach replaced Prince Carl as the chief agent for

Prince Carl Solms-Braunfels (1812–75) or to use his proper name, Friedrich Wilhelm Carl Ludwig Georg Alfred Alexander, Prince of Solms, Lord of Braunfels, Grafenstein, Münzenberg, Wildenfels, and Sonnenwalde, who was the first commissioner-general of the Adelsverein. Institute of Texan Cultures illustration no. 68-800

the *Verein*. Soon afterward, Meusebach founded Fredericksburg and made peace with the nearby Comanches. In January of 1847, he and forty of his men went to the Comanche camp on the San Saba River. To show his peaceful motives, Meusebach emptied his rifle in front of the Comanches. In turn, they respected his confidence and frankness. As a result, the Comanches agreed to allow the Germans to explore and settle in that area. It was the only treaty fully kept by both Indians and whites in Texas history.

From the Meusebach-Comanche agreement came the Fredericksburg Easter Fires tradition. Back home in Europe, the burning of such fires was a common practice. Meusebach made his treaty with the Comanches long before Easter; nevertheless, the Texas legend has it that when Meusebach traveled into Comanche territory, the Indians "placed guards around the town of Fredericksburg to ensure against the white man's treachery. They built signal fires on the hills overlooking the town. As long as the fires blazed high, the tribesmen in the distant camps knew that all was well. The children in the German settlement became frightened when they saw the fires. [So] a pioneer mother fabricated a story that it was only the Easter rabbit at work, boiling eggs in great cauldrons [pots] and then dying them with wildflowers gathered from the hills."[5]

As they settled in the Fredericksburg area, German Texans built houses of limestone, half-timber, or frame. Most had a large kitchen and a cellar, and "[m]any of the houses had half-stories where the

St. Mary's Church in Fredericksburg. Institute of Texan Cultures illustration no. 68-828

*John Offried Meusebach
(1812–97), also known as
Baron Otfried Hans
Freiherr von Meusebach, ca.
1888, by G. E. Wood.*
Institute of Texan Cultures
illustration no. 68-724

children slept, sometimes accessible by outside stairs. All of them
had large front and back porches called 'galleries.'"[6]

Fredericksburg's "Sunday Houses" were especially unique. They
do not exist anywhere else. As one scholar described them in 1928:

> The custom of building Sunday Houses began with a farmer who
> chose to buy a town lot. On it he built under his own vine and oak
> tree a box-like structure of lumber. Sometimes it had one room on
> the ground floor and a second surmounting it, with stairs leading up
> on the outside.
>
> To this city home the farmer comes on Sunday morning when
> his family is religiously inclined or on other times when the young
> folks want to attend the public balls that begin promptly at 2 P.M. in
> the various halls. When shopping is to be done, or a sick member of
> the family needs medical attention, in comes the farmer to his Sun-
> day House.

Of necessity, these temporary homes are furnished with one room often serving as kitchen, pantry, dining room, bedroom, and living room. And the thrifty farmer goes home with money in his pocket. He has not been forced to partake of boarding-house fare.[7]

Following the establishment of the settlements at Fredericksburg and New Braunfels, German immigration to Texas continued on an even larger scale with small family groups living close together. This led to the founding of the towns of Sisterdale, Boerne, and Comfort.

Two young girls, Eleanore and Anna Nagel, daughters of Louise and Herman Nagel of Cuero, Texas, ca. 1892. Institute of Texan Cultures illustration no. 99-828

The exterior of a Sunday House in Fredericksburg, Texas, ca. 1960. Institute of Texan Cultures illustration no. 81-463

Other Germans settled in San Antonio, Austin, Houston, Galveston, Castroville, Seguin, Victoria, and Indianola.

Such immigration and settlement in Texas was partly the result of small farmers in Germany being forced off their lands from the devastation of the potato blight, and the introduction of mass production left many skilled craftsmen jobless. More and more people chose to leave their homeland. So great was the immigration that between October, 1845, and April, 1846, some thirty-six ships brought more than five thousand Germans to Texas. By 1860 there were over twenty-four thousand foreign-born Germans in the state, making them the third-largest ethnic group after Anglo-Americans and African Americans.

For the recently arrived German immigrants settling in the Hill Country, problems lay ahead as Anglo settlers from the United States

▼▼▼

stampeded in to settle the premium lands owned by German immigrants. Bad feelings hit their peak on the eve of the Civil War. Small German farmers did not own slaves, and they felt a loyalty to the United States—not the Confederacy. As more German Texans spoke out against slavery, acts of violence occurred, including the hanging of four Germans near Grape Creek in Gillespie County. In 1862 the inhabitants of Fredericksburg viewed the Germans as such a threat that the town was placed under martial law and Confederate troops stationed there.

Between 1865 and 1890 over forty thousand Germans immigrated to Texas, settling throughout the state. Even with a decline in immigration in the early twentieth century, the pervasiveness of German influences in Texas was so widespread that by World War I anti-German sentiment became common. This caused public schools to stop teaching German.

Medina County residents, from left, Edmund and Louis Hutzler along with Louie Moehring, were photographed in the working dress of the turn-of-the-century cowboy, ca. 1900. Institute of Texan Cultures illustration no. 86-45

▼▼▼

Rosanna Dyer Osterman (1809–66)

Rosanna Dyer Osterman settled with her husband, Joseph, in Galveston during 1839. Joseph died accidentally from a pistol shot in 1861, but Rosanna carried on the family cotton export business. The family had many influential friends such as Sam Houston. Rosanna was responsible for bringing the first rabbi to Texas during the 1850s. Later she served as a Confederate spy during the American Civil War. Her espionage work began by serving as a nurse helping sick Union troops on Galveston Island. While nursing the sick men, she learned of a Union attack on Confederate forces scheduled for the middle of January, 1863. She relayed this information to Confederate troops on the mainland.

German immigrants represented a variety of religious faiths. Some were members of the Protestant faith such as the Lutherans, Methodists, Baptists, or Mennonites. Others were Roman Catholics or Jews. The German Catholics bore the brunt of widespread discrimination from English-speaking, non-Catholic neighbors. Generally, the Lutherans and Roman Catholics enjoyed dancing and drinking. The German Baptists, Mennonites, and Methodists avoided such entertainment. The Germans from the Christian groups built Gothic churches in Texas characterized by tall towers and magnificent painted interior walls.

A small number of German immigrants, who called themselves freethinkers, had no religious beliefs. These Germans had been among the intellectuals or artisans who supported the unsuccessful democratic revolutions in Europe during the middle of the nineteenth century. They left Germany to escape both political and religious oppression. A group of freethinkers settled in the town of Comfort in Kendall County, and from 1849 to 1892 no church was built in the town. Also as freethinkers they wanted nothing to do with the Confederacy during the Civil War. On the Nueces River about twenty miles from present-day Brackettville, the Confederates massacred more than half of the sixty-five freethinkers who were on their way to Mexico in 1862. A Union monument with its U.S. flag flying at half-mast in perpetuity was erected in Comfort in 1866 to honor these men—the only Union monument in a Confederate state.

Living in large numbers together in small towns isolated from other communities allowed the German Texans to maintain much of their culture. One cultural practice focused on the value of hard work, which was put forth in a popular folktale.

Once there was a farmer who was good, but he was very lazy and slept late and did not prosper. One day he was telling a friend his troubles. The friend, being very kind, did not wish to offend the farmer by telling him he was lazy. So he asked the farmer if he had ever seen a white sparrow. The farmer thought, and then said that he had not.

▼▼▼

"Would you like to see one?" asked the friend.

"Yes," said the farmer, "that would be a sight."

"Then," said the friend, "you must arise very early in the morning, for that is the only time when one may be seen."

So the farmer arose early the next morning, hoping to see the white sparrow. When he went out, he saw one of his workers walking off with a pail of milk. He saw another worker giving away a sack of grain. The farmer never saw a white sparrow, but he became more prosperous.[8]

Proverbs, or moral sayings, also provided a way to teach the value of hard work, and the Germans had several of them related to the work ethic including:

Well begun is half done.
Work makes life sweet.
What little Hans doesn't learn, big Hans will never learn.
Time brings wisdom.
What good is a pretty bowl if it is empty?[9]

Many of the special celebrations held by the German Texans such as those in Fredericksburg and the Gillespie County area are still observed by the numerous descendants of the German settlers.

St. Nicholas [the Patron Saint of Children's Feast Day] first visited the homes in Fredericksburg on the night of December 6 and occasionally thereafter until Christmas Eve. He left candy and fruit in little stockings hung from the bedposts and often peered through the casement to see whether or not the children of the household are obedient to their parents.

But the day of all days for children as well as for grown-ups was the 24th of December. It was then that at least one Santa Claus came to the homes. He entered about the time lights on the tree were lit. Every child was then asked to pray, "I am small; my heart is pure; no one shall abide there save Jesus alone."

The *Kindermaskenball* [children's masquerade ball], too, was a

The information helped to ensure the Confederate victory over Union forces at the January 1, 1863, Battle of Galveston.

Upon her death from an explosion aboard a Mississippi River steamboat in 1866, Rosanna bequeathed her fortune to charities. Her estate included funds for the eventual creation and maintenance of nondenominational widows', orphans', and sailors' homes in Galveston and the building of a synagogue in that city as well as one in Houston. Other funds went to Jewish schools and hospitals in New York City, Cincinnati, Philadelphia, and New Orleans, the latter her burial place.

Source: Based on Ruthe Winegarten and Cathy Schecter, *Deep in the Heart: The Lives and Legends of Texas Jews.* (Austin: Eakin Press, 1990).

▼▼▼

113

New Braunfels Girls Rifle Group. Institute of Texan Cultures illustration no. 68-887

great event. Practically all of the children in town gathered at one of the public halls for a frolic. Nymphs, butterflies, gnomes, witches, peasant maids, flower girls, and clowns skipped about merrily until 10 o'clock when they were whisked off home by their elders.[10]

The Germans were great ones for forming societies or social clubs. The *turnverein* movement began in Texas in 1850 by German political refugees who were practitioners of the gymnastics begun by Friedrich Jahn. Turnverein refers to a gymnastic or athletic club. Texas turnvereins were formed in Galveston in 1851, in Houston in 1854, in New Braunfels in 1855, in San Antonio in 1855, and in Comfort in 1860. The turnvereins promoted gymnastics and calisthenics as well as ninepin bowling. Adults had other entertainment such as the *Schützenfeste,* or shooting fests. Here the German Texans tested their skills at a shooting range. In between the shooting matches, a band played German music. The popular *Saengerfests,* or singing fests, began as events where local choral clubs sang German songs passed down from generation to generation—a tradition that continues today.

▼▼▼

Celebrations included, of course, good German beer and lots of good food. Some of the traditional favorites for the almost three million Texans of German descent include hot German sausage served on a stick along with hot German potato salad or sauerkraut salad and a cooled mug of beer.

Hot German Potato Salad
6 medium potatoes
¼ teaspoon pepper
pinch of salt
1 teaspoon celery seed
1 onion, diced
½ pound bacon, diced
2 tablespoons white vinegar
2 teaspoons sugar

Boil potatoes in salted water until tender. Peel and cube while still warm. Fry diced bacon until crisp and remove from skillet. Drain bacon fat, leaving about ½ cup in skillet. Add sugar, diced onion, vinegar, pepper, and celery seed. Add potatoes and bacon to skillet and heat.

A German band, probably in New Braunfels. Institute of Texan Cultures illustration no. 68-812

German Sauerkraut Salad

1 large onion, diced

1 cup sugar

2 cups sauerkraut, drained

¾ teaspoon salt

1 bell pepper, diced

1 large jar pimentos, diced

½ cup wine vinegar

1 large unpeeled apple, diced

1 cup celery, diced

¼ cup vegetable oil

Mix all ingredients and refrigerate overnight before serving. Makes about 12 servings.

THE WEND TEXANS

1870: 710 est.

1890: 500 est.

1900: no data

1910: no data

As part of a group of Wends, Johann Teinert remembers his voyage to Texas as a thirteen-year-old boy in 1854. The Wends, who left their homeland in Saxony in southeastern Germany, were Slavic conservative Lutherans who spoke a language similar to Polish, Czech, and Slovak.

In the year 1854 [580 of us] went on the railroad [from East Prussia] to Hamburg, Germany. . . . The ship owners chartered us a large ship, *Ben Nevis* by name. [Since] it was in the harbor of Liverpool, England, at the time . . . it was necessary that we travel on a freighter [from Hamburg] to England.

Then we arrived at Liverpool. There fourteen died. There we

waited until the ship was loaded. While we were sailing the cholera broke out and many became sick. Twenty-two died. How long we traveled no one knows. Because many were sick, we docked at Ireland, Queenstown harbor. There we all had to leave the ship and go on another one while our ship was washed and fumigated. This took a long time until everything was ready. Then we boarded [the *Ben Nevis*] and again traveled on.

(October 22, 1854) Thirty more died. . . . We sailed a long time, and then one afternoon a fierce storm came up which threatened to destroy the ship. . . .

[But] we sailed on. A few more still sick and some died. (Seven infants.) One night my mother also died. In the morning I went out on the deck and looked into the ocean and suddenly noticed how some men shoved a corpse into the water and how slowly it went down in the deep. This was my mother. This I could never forget.

We sailed onward until we saw sandy bars or dunes. There we held anchor for a couple of days because a big calm had set in and it was quite warm. One night a wind came up again, and so we traveled onward until we could see . . . Cuba. That meant that it was not very far to America.

We sailed onward until [on December 15] we came to land early in the morning. Everyone was glad. It did not take long and a ship met us. It showed us the way into the harbor [at Galveston Bay] and the place where our ship should anchor and where we should stay standing.[11]

When the Wends arrived in Galveston, they faced a yellow fever epidemic. Afraid of catching another sickness, they went to Houston. From there they walked to New Ulm and Industry where two of their leaders had gone ahead to purchase land for them.

They were not the first Wends to immigrate to Texas, but they came for the same reasons the earlier arrivals had. Many Wends in their homeland, especially during the 1700s, did not agree with the Prussian government, which wanted them to remain Roman Catholics rather than become members of the Lutheran Church. The government also discriminated against the Wends and demanded

Reverend Peter John Kilian with his daughter. Institute of Texan Cultures illustration no. 68-776

they speak only German and not their native language. The Wends were even denied citizenship and membership in guilds and often were restricted to living in certain parts of cities. Most became tenant or rent farmers, and when drought destroyed their farm crops, a few took the gamble and decided to immigrate. Leaders of the Wendish community decided that immigration was the only way to avoid the loss of their cultural, historical, religious, and linguistic heritage.

As a result, small groups of Wends went to Australia in the 1840s and settled near some Germans immigrants since the Wends could also speak German. A few others came to Texas in 1849 and lived in Austin County, again near some German immigrants. Another thirty-five Wends made their way to Texas and lived in the German communities of New Ulm and Industry.

The largest and last group of any size to arrive was the group aboard the *Ben Nevis* led by Peter John Kilian. With few belongings, the Wends in this group began to create a new life in what is now Lee County, about fifty miles from Austin. They cleared land, lived at first in dugout houses, and by 1860 had established the town of Serbin. They also built their Lutheran church—St. Paul's. It had its own parochial school where services and teaching could be conducted in Wendish as well as in German.

A hunting party of Wendish men near a barn on John Karisch farm near Warda in Fayette County. Institute of Texan Cultures illustration no. 83-129

▼▼▼

119

After having survived hardships such as malaria and typhoid, the Wends in Serbin finally began to prosper. They learned how to bring in the best crops of cotton, corn, sweet potatoes, and peanuts. Some became ranchers. Others would move south to Fayette County and farm or ranch there.

As time passed, most of the Wends assimilated into Texas culture. They would intermarry with other people and move elsewhere.[12] Nevertheless, some aspects of Wendish Texan culture have survived through the years. At Christmastime they would worship and enjoy the decorated tree prepared by the young people for the church. Like the Czechs, Poles, and other peoples of eastern European descent, Wends gave special significance to Easter, celebrating the event with elaborately decorated eggs. The decorated Wendish eggs often had Christian symbols such as

> stylized thorns, chalices and lambs—on the empty eggshells with a quill dipped in hot beeswax. After the wax hardened, the eggs were boiled in an onionskin dye, which the waxed designs resisted. The process resulted in Easter eggs of a deep red hue to symbolize the blood of Christ. . . . For the older girls of the community, gathering the Easter water *(jutrowna woda)* was a special event. The night before, or early Easter morning, the girls would go silently to the creek and fill a container with water. Then they sprinkled the water on their friends and livestock and sometimes even woke the sleeping household with it at daybreak in order to ensure good luck for the rest of the year.[13]

The Birds' Wedding was a custom especially for Wendish children that went as follows: "On January 25th the children would place empty plates and saucers outside, usually on fence posts and other high places to prevent raids by dogs and cats. The next morning the children would wake up to find the dishes filled with candy and nuts supposedly left for them by the birds. [The birds] were said to be celebrating their wedding and wanted to share their gifts with neighboring humans."[14]

▼▼▼

As was the case with other ethnic groups, weddings marked a rite of passage and were also very special occasions to the Wendish Texans. Weddings took place just after Sunday church services. In the mid-1800s the bride and her bridesmaids wore black dresses with floral headdresses. The black symbolized the hard life that lay ahead for the bride. However, by the 1890s the fashion for wedding dresses had changed. The bride and her bridesmaids wore gray, and by the

The wedding portrait of Theresia and Paul Lehmann, ca. 1900. Courtesy of Emily Ristau, Houston, Texas. Institute of Texan Cultures illustration no. 91-86

▼▼▼

early 1900s white wedding dresses were the style. After the wedding ceremony, a feast for the new husband and wife occurred.

> The wedding was followed by a heavy noon meal. The tables were laden with turkey and dressing, ham, beef and gravy, homemade noodles, boiled potatoes, fresh or canned vegetables, pickled beets and watermelon rind, fresh or stewed fruits, homemade bread with freshly churned butter, coffee or lemonade. That evening the leftovers were augmented with sausage, cheese, potato salad, more cakes, cookies and coffee. Traditionally at some point during these meals, a guest would reach under the table, pull off one of the bride's shoes and use it to take up a collection. The money was usually sent to a struggling young ministerial student, an orphanage, or some other worthy cause. . . .
>
> Throughout the day the bride and groom remained at the place of honor at the head table. Gifts were brought to them as well wishers gathered around to watch the packages being opened. At the conclusion of a midnight meal, the maid of honor removed the bride's veil, and the couple was free to mingle with the guests.
>
> Outside, a noisy crowd ringing cowbells and drumming on washtubs gathered for a shivaree. The bride and groom would greet the revelers and invite them in for refreshment. Those guests who chose to spend the remaining hours of the night were bedded down on the floor. When morning came the bride cooked a breakfast of pork sausage, eggs, homemade bread, cake and coffee. Such festivities usually lasted several days—until the last survivor could no longer bear the sight of food. One assumes the bride and groom were equally eager to see the guests depart![15]

Just as they were a small ethnic group within their homeland, the Wends were also a small group in Texas. Over the years they married neighbors with ethnically different backgrounds. Nevertheless, they retained many of the traditions of their homeland including recipes. A treat of homemade noodles was a favorite among them.

▼▼▼

Wendish Noodles

6 eggs
6 tablespoons of cream
1 teaspoon salt
4½ cups flour
1 quart water
2 tablespoons salt

Combine eggs, cream, and salt. Beat thoroughly. Stir in flour gradually to form dough that can be made into a ball. Knead on floured surface for 10 minutes. Divide dough into four portions. On a lightly floured surface, roll each portion, stretching the dough until paper thin. Let dry 30 minutes. Cut into strips the width of the noodles desired. Drop into boiling salted water and cook about 6 minutes.

Mrs. A. B. Stephens, Evelyn and James Kotula, and Mrs. Ed Kotula in traditional Polish hats. Institute of Texan Cultures illustration no. 72-2

Drain. Can be added to 2 quarts chicken broth flavored with diced celery, onions, and parsley for a wonderful soup.

THE POLISH TEXANS

1870: 448
1890: 1,591
1900: 3,348
1910: no data

Clothing worn by some of the first Poles who came to Texas during the mid-1800s caused a sensation among others. One observer noted that many of the Polish women had "what at that time were regarded as very short skirts, showing their limbs two or three inches above the ankles. Some had on wooden shoes, and almost without exception they had broad-brimmed, low-crowned black felt hats, nothing like the hats then worn in Texas. They also wore blue jackets of heavy woolen cloth, falling below the waist, and gathered into folds at the back with a band of the same material."

Those "short" skirts worn by Polish Texan women caused their Roman Catholic priest, Father Leopold Moczygemba, to write family members in Poland who planned to move to Texas. "Don't take any country dresses for Hanka, because she will not need them here. Our country dresses are the reason that the native people make fun of us and they cause sin."[16]

Polish immigrants encountered other discrimination and prejudice. The differences they brought with them, whether dress or religion or language, caused others to speak unkindly about them and avoid the new arrivals. Thus most new Polish immigrants settled in communities with others from their homeland.

Rattlesnakes, too, posed a problem for many of the early Polish Texans as they did not have such reptiles in their homeland. One of those early Polish settlers noted that in Texas, "There was tall grass

▼▼▼

everywhere, so that if anyone took a few steps he was soon lost to sight. Every step of the way you would meet rattlesnakes. . . . And several died of snakebites. . . . Everybody without exception had to carry a stick, hoe, or pitchfork wherever he took a step as a protection against snakes."

In one memorable encounter with a rattlesnake, Father Moczygemba "planned a dinner to welcome to Texas a group of newly arrived Polish immigrants. They complained to him about the conditions they had found in Texas, but Father Leopold succeeded in calming them. Then, just as he was serving the group, a big rattlesnake tumbled down from the rafters onto the table. As a Pole recounted the story, 'How they shrieked until they could get out of the hut!'"[17]

People facing such problems who came to Texas during the 1800s had many reasons for leaving their homeland. Between 1772 and 1914 the Poles had no real country. Poland had been divided between Russia, Prussia, and Austria. Poles were even forbidden to speak Polish. To overcome that, some Poles staged unsuccessful revolutions in the 1790s and again from 1830 to 1831 against Russian rule. Polish men resented having to serve in either the Russian, Prussian, or Austrian armies. Moreover, a number of disasters struck in Poland during the 1850s. People died from typhoid and cholera while others starved due to floods destroying their crops. Then in 1863 another rebellion of Poles against Russian rule failed.

Poles with enough money moved elsewhere in Europe. Those without much income decided to come to America and found their way to Texas. Simon Weiss, who had come in 1833, supported the Texas Revolution and became a successful businessman in the Nacogdoches area. Other Poles who fought in the Texas Revolution included Michael Debricki, Francis Petrussewicz and his brother, Adoph, John Kornicky, and Joseph Schrusneki. All were killed in the Goliad Massacre on March 27, 1836. Another Pole, Felix Wardzinski, fought with Sam Houston at the San Jacinto battle.

The early Polish immigration to Texas served as a foundation for other Poles. Indeed, the major Polish settlement in Texas became

Father Leopold Moczygemba (1824–91) was born in the Upper Silesian village of Plužnica. Institute of Texan Cultures illustration no. 68-1231a

the first permanent Polish colony in America. Founded by Franciscan priest Leopold Moczygemba, the colony began in 1854 at Panna Maria, near the junction of the San Antonio River and Cibolo Creek in Karnes County. Arriving from Upper Silesia in Prussian Poland, Father Moczygemba came to Texas when he was twenty-six years old. At first he served the German settlers of New Braunfels and the French Alsace at Castroville. His letters back home persuaded nearly eight hundred Poles to leave their homeland for Texas. Some died during the long trip from Poland to Panna Maria, with the remainder joining Father Moczygemba to create a lasting colony.

In 1855 the settlers founded the state's first Polish Roman Catholic Church at Panna Maria, and in 1866 they began the first Polish school, St. Joseph's. A second group of seven hundred Poles arrived in 1855, and a third group of five hundred arrived three years later

Painting of the Black Madonna, or Our Lady of Çestochowa, given by members of the Panna Maria Church for the new church at Çestochowa. Institute of Texan Cultures illustration no. 74-1191

Exterior of the John Gawlik residence that was built in 1858 at Panna Maria. Institute of Texan Cultures illustration no. 82-161a

Mrs. Felix Urbanczyk and Mrs. Ben Urbanczyk with a gun preparing to shoot a fox. Institute of Texan Cultures illustration no. 68-2336

▼▼▼

and joined the original Polish settlers. By 1873 a group of Polish farm families formed the Çestochowa community, five miles upstream from Panna Maria on the Cibolo Creek. The members of the church at Panna Maria presented the new parish a large painting of the Black Madonna, or Our Lady of Çestochowa, the patroness of Poland. After the Civil War, many Galician Poles who lived along the Russian border on small farming plots came to settle along the Brazos River and at Bremond in Robertson County.

The stone or oak-frame homes with a long pitched roof that the Poles built in central Texas during the mid- to late 1800s looked like those from Upper Silesia in Poland. In their native homeland, Poles built such roofs so the snow would slide off. The Texas homes, though, added porches facing south to catch the faint breeze from the Gulf of Mexico.

The John Dugosh family making molasses in Bandera, Texas, ca. 1900– 15. Institute of Texan Cultures illustration no. 68-1210

In addition to concerns about their dress and rattlesnakes, Polish Texans faced numerous other problems. There were attacks by Indians on Poles living in the Bandera area. They were also the victims of prejudice, mean jokes, and unscrupulous business dealings. In several instances after the Civil War, cowboys wearing hats and smoking cigarettes entered Polish church services. In 1869 one band of cowboys even shot up the town of Panna Maria. When the Poles threatened to defend themselves, the harassment stopped with the help of U.S. soldiers from San Antonio.

Nevertheless, the Polish Texans persisted. With firm determination they succeeded in their economic endeavors. Most were farmers; others became ranchers. Some formed businesses both in the smaller towns and in the larger urban areas such as San Antonio. By 1900 over sixteen thousand Poles along with their descendants made Texas their home. They established churches and founded or settled in such places as Cestohowa (originally Çestochowa), Kosciusko, Falls City, Polonia, New Waverly, Brenham, Marlin, Anderson, Bryan, Chappell Hill, St. Hedwig, White Deer, Navasota, Bremond, Plantersville, Thurber, Bandera, Cotulla, Yorktown, and McCook.

Polish Texans also continued to maintain traditions from their homeland including the wedding ceremony. One example comes from the numerous Poles who worked at the Thurber coal mines. During the 1880s the Polish men did much of the underground work before the mines closed in 1921.

Before the service in the Thurber Catholic Church, the bride and groom in their festive dress were driven about the town to show off their finery. After the wedding service, the couple rode to the bride's parents for a magnificent wedding feast. Frequently, hundreds of guests attended the celebrations, which sometimes lasted for three or four days. When night came it was time for dancing either in the parents' home or in the dance hall located on "Polander Hill." These dances also served as a means of securing money for the new couple. In order to dance with the bride, a man would throw a coin, trying to break a big, thick dinner plate. If he failed to shatter the plate, he

Clara Rakowitz and Pete Kaczmarek in their wedding clothes at St. Hedwig in 1868. Institute of Texan Cultures illustration no. 68-1200

lost his money and his opportunity to dance. Most of the guests chose to throw silver dollars, which were more likely to break the plates. As one historian of Thurber wrote, "It was not uncommon for the newly married couple to receive three or four hundred dollars by the time the celebration was over."[18]

Their Christmas celebration, which lasted from December 24 through January 6, included another tradition brought from their homeland. Before the Christmas Eve dinner, the head of the household served everyone part of a small, flat oblong wafer, an *oplateck*, that was blessed by the priest. It had a nativity scene impressed on it symbolizing love, friendship, and forgiveness.

Christmas Eve dinner usually involved the preparation of fish. Herring was coated in flour and fried. Trout or carp were steamed in vinegar. Perch was covered with egg or olive sauce before being heated. Salmon was sautéed in oil. That was followed with beet soup, mushroom patties, almond soup, hunter's stew, a biscuit, and honey or seed cakes. The main course for Christmas Day was goose soup mixed with noodles, raisins, and prunes. After dinner, someone played Santa Claus (Star Man) and asked the children how they had behaved during the year. Following that, the family attended Midnight Shepherd's Mass.

Easter is equally important to Polish Texans. In addition to the celebration at church, there is the Easter Feast with its colored Easter eggs, a traditional eastern European practice. Ornamented in three ways, the eggs may be painted in solid colors, scratched with a sharp instrument to form a design on the surface, or batiked with marvelous traditional designs called *pisanki*. It is for the practice of *pisanki* that the Poles are most famous. Decorated with complex lines, dots, and symbols, the *pisanki* are truly works of art with no two alike.

After being blessed by the priest, the eggs serve several purposes. They are central to the opening of the Easter Feast and are given away and sometimes treasured for years as good luck charms. Years ago young Polish girls would give as many as one hundred eggs to favored suitors as signs that their attentions would be welcomed.[19]

One of the traditional recipes of the 237,557 (1990) Texans of Polish descent is for a cold beet soup.[20]

Polish Easy Barszcz *(Beet Soup)*
12 medium beets
1 medium onion, sliced
1 quart water
juice of 1 lemon
1 tablespoon sugar
salt and pepper
2 cups bouillon
½ cup sour cream

Wash and peel beets. Cook beets and onion in water until beets are tender. Add lemon juice, sugar, salt, and pepper. Let stand overnight. Strain. Add bouillon and sour cream. Reheat and serve with *uszka.*

Polish Uszka
Meatless Filling:
1 tablespoon chopped onion
3 tablespoons butter
2 cups cooked chopped mushrooms
salt and pepper

Fry onion in butter until brown. Add mushrooms and fry very slowly for 10 minutes. Add salt and pepper. Cool.

Wrapping:
2 cups flour
1 egg
1 cup water
½ teaspoon salt
2 tablespoons mashed potatoes

Mound flour on a breadboard. Beat egg slightly with water and salt. Pour carefully into mound of flour. Mix and add mashed potatoes. Knead until dough becomes elastic.

▼▼▼

Cover and let stand about 10 minutes in a warm place. For easier handling, divide dough in half. Roll out very thin and cut in 2" squares. Place ½ teaspoon of filling on each side of square. Moisten edge with water, fold over, and press edges together. Join two upper corners. Drop into salted boiling water and cook until they float to top.

THE CZECH TEXANS

1870: 781
1890: 3,215
1900: 9,204
1910: no data

The Hanicak family—Jan, Katerina, and two of their children, Jan, Jr., and Annie—came to Texas in 1906. Jan, a cottager who farmed small plots of land, had to serve in the Austrian Army like most young adult males in the region that later became Czechoslovakia. At that time, Austria controlled the area where the Hanicak family lived. A cavalry horse injured Jan while he was in the army, and he killed the horse in self-defense. Since there were more men than horses in the army, he was sent to prison as punishment for killing the horse.

Jan's brother, Peter, and his family had already immigrated to a Czech community in Bessmay, Texas, located thirty-seven miles north of Beaumont in south central Jasper County. Peter worked in a sawmill in nearby Deweyville. When Peter wrote about how good life was in Texas, Jan and Katerina began to save their money to immigrate to Deweyville.

They left from Novy Hrozenkov in August, 1906, taking only two small trunks of clothes with them. Jan, Jr., only eighteen months old, was sick during most of the boat trip. In fact, almost everyone on the ship got seasick except Annie, their daughter. She took meals to some people too sick to get their own food. The trip took twenty-

Jan, Katerina, and Jan Hanicak, Jr., in Silsbee, Texas. Courtesy of Marguerite L. Kownslar, San Antonio, Texas. Institute of Texan Cultures illustration no. 102-66

six days, and they arrived in Galveston, Texas, on Annie's eighth birthday.

The family moved to Bessmay with their relatives, and Jan got a job at the nearby sawmill in Kirby. The Hanicaks liked their new home, but life was difficult. Although fluent and literate in Czech, German, and Russian, they could not speak English. Some children in school made fun of Annie and took her things. Once, the teacher

Students at the Chromcik School in Fayetteville, Texas. Institute of Texan Cultures illustration no. 72-791

asked Annie if she took a pencil from another student, which she had not, but the only English word she knew at the time was "yes," so that was how she answered. The teacher punished her.

After the Hanicaks had been in Texas for several years, Jan, Sr., hurt his leg in an accident at the sawmill. The men who worked with him put a tourniquet on his leg and took him to the closest hospital about thirty miles away. The doctor amputated his leg because the tourniquet had been left on too long. After that, money was scarce, so Katerina took in roomers and cooked meals for them, converting their home into a boardinghouse. Annie and Jan, Jr., helped too by running errands for the neighbors and doing odd jobs. At thirteen, Jan, Jr., quit school and went to work full time at the sawmill. The family continued to work very hard to save enough

▼▼▼

money to buy a home. Finally, a few years after Jan, Sr., died, Katerina was able to get her own home.

Jan, Jr., who had taken the English name of John, proudly gained American citizenship. In 1935 he married Scottish-Swiss Texan Margaret McGhee of Brownwood, Texas. Her ancestors had settled on part of Stephen F. Austin's colony during the early 1820s. Margaret graduated at the head of her class from Brownwood (Texas) High School and Daniel Baker College, a Presbyterian school in Brownwood. Margaret was on Daniel Baker's female basketball and softball teams and was the only woman, a sprinter, on the college track team. Her first teaching job was in Silsbee, Texas, where she taught Latin, ancient history, and algebra.

While in Silsbee, Margaret met and became engaged to John Hanicak who at the time worked for the Santa Fe Railroad. After a five-year engagement, they secretly married. They kept their marriage a secret because female teachers in her school district were not permitted to marry. Soon afterward, she and John moved to Port Neches, Texas.

In Port Neches, John worked at the Texas Company (Texaco) refinery as a machinist, but the Hanicaks also had their own farm. John became an organic farmer, never using insecticides, and Margaret, no longer teaching, learned to milk cows and do other farm chores. John became so Americanized that he would not allow the family to purchase anything not made by an American labor union. He also would not teach any of his children to speak Czech. However, John spoke Czech with his old friends and, when he could, listened to Czech music and ate traditional Czech foods.

Annie Hanicak married Frank Foyt, a farmer and fellow immigrant from Czechoslovakia. While Frank had learned English, he had his children learn Czech along with English, telling them "a calf speaks the same language as the cow."[21]

The language problem facing the Hanicak family was also typical of what many early Czech immigrants faced upon arriving in Texas. Most Czech Texans first banded together forming their own communities or lived in German towns where they could speak the

John Pliska
(1879–1956)

John Valentine Pliska was born in Tyne, Moravia, and worked helping his father in his blacksmith and carriage shops. During his required service in the Austro-Hungarian Army, he attended a balloon and glider school in Bavaria. His family came to Texas and settled in Flatonia where he worked on farms in Central Texas.

After working around Midland as a repairman, he returned to Flatonia and married Louise Hundle. In 1907 he and his brother-in-law, John Hundle, bought a blacksmith shop in Midland, Texas. A year later he began planning to build an airplane. After seeing a Wright Brothers' Model B plane on a cross-country flight, he really got busy and hired Gary Coggin, a local automobile mechanic, to help him.

language. Czech Texans learned both English and Czech in their Roman Catholic or public schools until just after 1900.

Many of the Czechs who came to Texas were from Bohemia and Moravia with a lesser number from Silesia. One of the earliest Czech immigrants to Texas was Frederick Lemsky. He played the fife at the battle of San Jacinto. Another early Czech arrival was Anthony Michael Dignowity. He visited Texas in 1835 and returned in 1846 during which time he served as a medical doctor in the Mexican War. So desperately were doctors needed in San Antonio that he stayed and made it his home. Another important Czech immigrant was Josef Bergmann, a Protestant minister. He settled in Cat Spring located in Austin County. From there he wrote letters back to his homeland, encouraging other Czechs to move to Texas.

Bergmann's letters inspired Josef Lesikar of Bohemia. In 1851 he sent sixteen families on their way to Texas. Unfortunately, the ship they took from Liverpool, England, to New Orleans was dangerously overcrowded with very unhealthy living conditions. As a result, almost all aboard were ill when they arrived in New Orleans. Some died there before the others went on to Galveston. Of the seventy-four Czechs who set out on the trip, only thirty-eight survived to reach Austin County.

Lesikar then led his own group of seventeen families to New Ulm, Texas, in 1852. As he later wrote, "Our trip across the ocean lasted seven weeks. After a short rest at Galveston we were taken by a riverboat to Houston, from whence we proceeded by ox team into the interior. This part of the journey lasted a full fourteen days although it was only a distance of sixty miles. . . . A well built house was not to be seen, only log cabins in which there was not a single nail; in place of glass windows there were but holes in the wall, the entrance covered with woven twigs served the purpose of a door; planks, nails, pieces of iron were considered rarity. In our settlement only half of us had a team and wagon."[22]

Despite their difficulties, the group worked hard and became the first of many successful Czech Texan farmers. The beginning of a great migration of Czechs to Texas began in 1851. By 1900 they

▼▼▼

John Pliska, standing, and Gray Coggin with the Pliska airplane at Polo Field in Midland, ca. 1909. Institute of Texan Cultures illustration no. 72-1809

After spending fifteen hundred dollars on the engine, Pliska completed his plane in 1912, and the open-cockpit craft made mostly from buggy and windmill parts flew over the Polo Grounds at the Quien Sabe Ranch, southeast of Midland.

Pliska continued to work as a master blacksmith in Midland where his plane was stored in the rafters of his blacksmith shop from 1912 to 1962. The plane has now been restored and is on display at the Midland International Airport.

Source: Julia Cauble Smith, "John Valentine Pliska," *Handbook of Texas Online,* http://www.tsha.utexas.edu/handbook/online/index.html (Feb. 13, 2002).

had become the largest eastern European immigrant group to settle in Texas.

Most Czechs came to Texas for the same reasons as the Hanicak family. Austria, which controlled most of the regions inhabited by Czech people, drafted unwilling young men into the army to fight in European wars. Poor Czech families also lacked funds to acquire additional property in their homeland. As a result, many found Texas appealing with its land of rich black soil. It seemed an ideal place to create their family farms. By 1860 the first Czech settlements in Austin and Fayette Counties had extended from central Austin County west to Fayette County and north to the edge of Washington County. By the 1890s and early 1900s Czechs had also moved into the North Texas community of Rowena in Runnels County and Bomarton in Baylor County, eventually establishing nearly three hundred Czech communities in the state.[23]

A majority of the Czech immigrants were Roman Catholics with a minority of United Brethren, Presbyterians, Methodists, and Baptists. The United Brethren trace their origins to Jan Hus, a Czech Protestant of the fifteenth century. He sought a more simple Christian

Anita Bartosh, center, *with two younger attendants, dressed for first Commun-ion at Catholic church in Granger, ca. 1905.* Institute of Texan Cultures illus-tration no. 97-741

life and stressed education and nonviolence. A lesser number of Czechs were freethinkers and were not part of any religious group.

Czech Texan Catholics built wonderful painted churches that remain today. The ones at Ammansville, southeast of La Grange, and at High Hill, southwest of La Grange, are typical. St. John the Baptist

Church, a wooden church in Ammansville was built in 1879, but the church that stands on the site today, the "Pink Church," is the third church built on the site. A hurricane destroyed the first church in 1909, and a fire in 1917 burned the second one. Architect Leo M. J. Dielmann built the Nativity of Mary, Blessed Virgin Catholic Church of red brick at High Hill in 1906. The decorative painting was done on canvas and then glued to the interior wood walls. Traditional Czech church weddings were held there with elaborate preparations.

First, the young couple had to rent land on which to farm. Next, the all-important wedding feast required the raising of additional chickens, turkeys and geese, and perhaps an extra calf and hog. Well in advance of the celebration the couple selected their attendants. The groom would choose two of his groomsmen to dress in their Sunday best and ride around from house-to-house extending formal invitations.

A few days before the ceremony friends of the family would gather to assist in the preparations. There had to be not only food for the feast, but plenty for the guests to take home. Numerous kegs of beer were also provided. Much of the baking was done two or three days ahead of time, but the meat was usually cooked on the morning of the wedding. Breakfast was then served to the couple, their attendants and immediate families. A groom was not permitted to see his bride in her wedding dress before two o'clock in the afternoon, when the guests gathered in the church parlor. On the arrival of the bride and her parents, a man called the *starosta* stepped forward and presented her to the groom. He admonished the groom to be kind, gentle and worthy; and the bride to be moral, obedient and submissive. Both were told to honor their parents. After this came the procession to the sanctuary.

Following the ceremony, the crowd returned to the bride's home for the feast. Perhaps they would be stopped by friends who would stretch a ribbon across the road and ask for a donation. The proceeds might be given either to the newlyweds, or to the musicians— who had doubtless earned it! At the reception the bridesmaids would

On August 16, 1910, Joe Machu, left, *married Tracy Zetak with his brother John,* right, *marrying Frances Kopecky.* Institute of Texan Cultures illustration no. 98-185

pin on each guest a sprig of rosemary, which symbolized fidelity and constancy. Sometimes a collection would be taken up to buy a cradle for the first child. Then came a virtual orgy of eating, drinking, dancing and visiting.[24]

While the traditional Czech weddings are rarely performed today, other celebrations occur at which Czech descendants might wear the traditional folk dress. Most of the first Czechs who came to Texas abandoned the traditional folk clothing, but as their descendants became more interested in the old-country ways, they began to wear the costumes at special events. The women wear a "skirt in a multicolored pattern or solid hue; a vest, usually black with gold or lace trim; a blouse with a large collar, ruffles on the sleeves and embroidery all over; and a brightly decorated cap. The men are no less brilliantly attired. Their pants are nearly always a solid shade, but decorated or patterned to suit the individual gentleman's taste."[25]

▼▼▼

The Czech oral tradition has also survived through the telling of folktales. Some stories explain the origins of things.

A turtle, for instance, was once a woman who hid under a tub when a storm was coming. After the storm had passed the woman found that she could not remove the tub. It had become a shell grown to her. That is why a turtle always hides when a rain or a storm is coming. . . .

A little black-eyed pea once saw something very funny. It laughed so heartily that it popped. Quickly, the little pea ran to a tailor and asked to be sewed up with white thread. The tailor, having no white thread, sewed it up with black thread. That is why the pea has a little black spot on it.[26]

The Czechs also brought with them the *sokol* (meaning, literally, falcon) with its motto "A Sound Mind in a Sound Body." A carryover from Czechoslovakia, the Texas *Sokol* promoted physical training and Czech singing and dancing. Especially evident among the Czech Texan musical heritage are the polka and the waltz. One of the earliest Texas groups to preserve them was led by Frank Baca. He organized his own orchestra in 1892 at Bordovice near Fayetteville.

Part-time mail carriers, left to right, *Joe Huser, Frank Martinet, and Edward Bartosh, on motorcycles in Granger.* Institute of Texan Cultures illustration no. 98-194

Girls from the Sokol *conduct an exercise during July Fourth picnic at Lonnie Hill's River Boom by Willis Creek near Granger, ca. 1920.* Institute of Texan Cultures illustration no. 98-179

His descendants have carried on the family's musical tradition. But as times have changed, so have such bands, adding country western music to the performances. What evolved from this has come to be known as "polk-a-billy."

Traditional Czech dance is especially evident in the *beseda,* which is still performed at local festivals. It calls for multiple circles of four couples. They dance the old favorites from the Bohemian, Moravian, Silesian, and Slovak cultures.

Decorated Easter eggshells, a longtime eastern European custom, are also part of the Czech Texan heritage. A small hole is poked in each end of the egg with a needle. Next, a person blows in one end to push out the white and yoke of the egg. The egg is then ready to be dyed and decorated. A sharp instrument is used to scratch a design on the shell. The designs are many. Flowers, for example, represent farewell gifts. Others feature good luck poems. Four eggs with religious designs represent the seasons of the year. A young girl might give a decorated egg to a boy she likes.

Equally as well known as their music, dance, and decorated eggs are the traditional *koláč.* Now known as *kolaches,* the pastry is enjoyed by the more than 168,023 (1990) Texans of at least partial Czech descent.[27]

Kolaches
1 stick margarine, melted
2 eggs
2 cups warm milk
cup sugar
2 packages dry yeast
2 teaspoons salt
½ cup warm water
8 to 9 cups flour
2 teaspoons sugar

Combine margarine and milk in a saucepan and heat until the margarine is melted. Mix yeast, warm water, and 2 teaspoons sugar in a large mixing bowl. Beat the eggs in a cup with a fork, add to margarine and milk mixture in the saucepan, and then add it all to the yeast mixture in the large bowl. Add ½ cup sugar and salt. Gradually add sifted flour to make a stiff dough. Usually 8½ cups of flour is sufficient. Let the mixture sit 15 minutes. Knead until

The first Czech band in Texas was organized in Fayetteville by Frank Baca in 1882. Institute of Texan Cultures illustration no. 68-2366

▼▼▼

145

smooth and let rise 50 minutes in a warm place until double in bulk. After dough has risen, divide it into egg-size portions with a spoon and form balls. Place on an oiled baking sheet about an inch apart and brush with melted butter. Let rise until light and then make an indentation in each ball for fruit. Sprinkle with *posipka* topping.

Fillings for Kolaches

Prune Filling:
1 pound cooked prunes
3 tablespoons melted butter
1½ cups sugar vanilla or cinnamon

Apricot Filling:
1 pound dry apricots, cooked
½ teaspoon almond flavor
3 tablespoons melted butter

Put dried fruit in saucepan with water and cook until thickened. Add remaining ingredients and cool. When cool, spread on kolaches.

Posipka Topping
1 cup sugar
½ cup flour

Combine ingredients. Sprinkle over fruit filling. Let the kolaches rise again about twenty minutes or until light to the touch. Bake at 450° for 15 minutes. Remove from oven. Butter each kolache again before removing from pan onto a wire cooling rack or large board. Makes about 6 dozen. Prunes or apricots are the fruits generally used for kolaches. They are cooked, sweetened, pureed, and usually mildly spiced with cinnamon or nutmeg.

▼▼▼

THE HUNGARIAN TEXANS

1870: 46
1890: 228
1900: 593
1910: 926

The story of the Nagy family is a typical one among the Hungarian families who immigrated to Texas during the nineteenth century. John Nagy served for twelve years as a sergeant in the Hungarian Army and then became a postmaster. During that time he married Kristina Botka. The couple had nine children, six of whom lived to adulthood. Their oldest son, Joseph, at age eighteen, was the first member of the family to move to Texas. He did not wish to serve in the Hungarian Army and sought a better way of life. In 1897 he immigrated to Ellis County with the Hungarian family of Frank Szénási. Three years later Joseph's father, John, and three of his siblings arrived in Texas. When John had saved enough money, he sent for Kristina and their other children. Kristina brought her goose-down comforters, pillows, and handmade linens.

Annie, the family's fifteen-year-old daughter, recalled her arrival with her mother and sister at Galveston on October 14, 1900. They witnessed the devastation of the great hurricane, which had destroyed much of Galveston and killed over six thousand people the month before their arrival. Because food was still scarce in Galveston, Annie, her sister, and mother managed to buy only some bananas, which they thought were long cantaloupes. Annie recalled that "on top of the railroad station there were bedsteads and other furniture that . . . had been washed there by the flood." On the train bound for Ellis County, she recalled that between "Galveston and Houston on each side of the train tracks, which were higher than other terrain, there was water, and many dead cows and other animals were on top of trees, along with the boughs and much debris."[28]

Once settled, the Nagy family worked hard to become successful cotton farmers on their land near the Ellis-Navarro County line.

However, John and Kristina never learned to speak English. Instead, they let their sons and daughters do the necessary translations for them when necessary.

Joseph married Elizabeth Szénási, a member of the Hungarian family he had traveled with to Texas. They, too, prospered as cotton farmers in the Ellis-Navarro County area. Their grandson, named after Joseph, served as a president of the state bar of Texas.

One of Elizabeth's favorite dishes was *retes,* a Hungarian pastry. At age seventy-one she gave the recipe for the dessert to a newspaper reporter in Alice, Texas.

> Proud to say that she "never bought a loaf of bread in her life," Mrs. Nagy, who was born in Hungary in 1885, added that "I made all my lard and noodles." Similar to German strudel, the Hungarian *retes* were made by stretching the dough instead of rolling it out. Consisting of flour . . . lard, and salt mixed with cold water, the dough had to be worked thoroughly and then stretched, without breaks, until it

The Joseph Nagy family with daughter Elizabeth, left, *and son Joseph,* right, *at their home in Millett.* Institute of Texan Cultures illustration no. 86-35

was paper thin, or large enough to cover a dining table. Filling made of just about anything, except runny jelly, could be used. Mrs. Nagy's favorite was a mixture of ground pecans, sugar, and fine breadcrumbs, but peaches, apricots, or apples could be added. Then, with the table-cloth beneath used for shaping, the thin dough was rolled into sausage shapes, which were immediately browned in the oven. The crust was flaky, and the *retes* could be kept for days without becoming tough. Mrs. Nagy also raised her own poppies and ground the seeds in a coffee grinder. She mixed poppy seeds with sugar, pecans, and raisins for her *retes.*[29]

The Nagys were among the few adventurous Hungarians to arrive in Texas before the twentieth century. Hungary, located in east central Europe, includes people of several ethnic groups who have had difficulty living together. The numerous wars during the 1800s caused many to seek a life elsewhere. Anton Lochmar came in 1833 and opened a hotel in San Antonio. Gottfried Joseph Petmecky arrived in Texas during 1845 and operated a gunsmith shop in Austin. He became famous for inventing the spring-shank steel spur. When a cowboy was thrown from his horse, the Petmecky spur would open and fall away. This eliminated the risk of breaking an ankle or leg. Another early Hungarian arrival in 1845 was Rudolph Schorobiny. He became a well-respected farmer and Texas Ranger in Medina County.

Still, it was not until the end of the ill-fated Hungarian attempt to become an independent country in 1849 that more Hungarians came to Texas. In the 1840s Hungary included parts of present-day Romania, Slovakia, Bohemia, Ukraine, Slovenia, Yugoslavia, Croatia, Germany, and Serbia. All were under the rule of the Austrian Hapsburgs. Unhappy with Austrian domination, many Hungarians unsuccessfully fought to create an independent state during 1848 and 1849. They failed when Russians and Croatians joined forces with the Austrians to defeat the rebelling Hungarians. More Hungarians left Europe and came to the United States—some of them to Texas.

One of the first of those rebelling Hungarians to arrive in Texas was László Újházi. He was born in 1795 on his family's estate in Upper Hungary, now Czechoslovakia. A member of the noble class, he supported Hungarian independence from Austria. When Újházi became a leader of the Hungarian exiles, he planned to create a colony of Hungarians in Iowa. When that failed, he decided to move the colony to Texas. The settlers in the colony were to remain in Texas until Hungary became free of Austrian domination. Since his dream of an independent Hungary did not occur during his lifetime, he remained in the Olmos Basin near the town of San Antonio. There he and his wife, Teréz Várady Szakmáry, ranched, put in a vineyard with cuttings from Hungary, and encouraged other Hungarians to move to Texas, though less than a few hundred did so in the mid-1800s.

A lifelong opponent of slavery, Újházi supported the Union during the American Civil War, serving as an ambassador to Italy for President Abraham Lincoln. After returning to his home in Texas when the Civil War ended, Újházi helped form the Republican Party in his adopted state. He died at his Olmos Basin home on March 7, 1870—a hero of democracy.

The next important migration of Hungarians to Texas occurred in the latter part of the nineteenth and early part of the twentieth centuries. During that time Hungary was overpopulated, which caused about five hundred Hungarians to seek a new life in the Lone Star State. Like the Nagys and Újházi, most went into agriculture.

A majority of the Hungarian immigrants were Roman Catholics, while others were Moslems. One aspect of the Hungarian Christian culture focused on the Christmas tree. According to custom, the children did not take part in decorating the tree. They were told that the Christ child and the angels brought the tree and presents before Christmas Eve. At the appropriate time, a bell signaled to the children that the tree was ready for them to view.

Especially important in decorating the Christmas tree was to use *szalon cukor*, a special Hungarian Christmas candy that many of the 30,234 (2000) Texans of Hungarian descent still enjoy.[30]

▼▼▼

László Újházi (1795–1870), Hungary's first political refugee from the Hungarian Revolution (1848–49) to come to Texas. Institute of Texan Cultures illustration no. 86-487

Szalon Cukor *Candy*

Measure 4 cups sugar into an aluminum pot. Add 1 cup cold water. Boil ingredients over medium heat about 20–25 minutes until mixture thickens. Do not stir mixture while it is heating. Test mixture for thickness by inserting a loop of thin wire into the pan. If it is possible to blow a sugary bubble with the mixture adhering to the wire loop, then the syrup is ready to be removed from the heat. If not,

▼▼▼

continue the heating process. While the candy syrup is still cooking, prepare two large platters (flat surfaces) onto which the mixture will be poured. Rinse the platters with cold water leaving surfaces damp. When the mixture is ready, remove candy from the stove. Divide it into two portions right away. To one portion add ⅓ cup of ground hazelnuts or pecans and one teaspoon of vanilla. Start stirring that portion right away with an electric mixer. To the second portion, meanwhile, add 1 teaspoon of vanilla and 1 teaspoon cocoa or mocha coffee powder. Stir with a wooden spoon until mixture hardens. Both portions should be stirred until the candy hardens but with enough suppleness left that it can be poured onto the platters. After the candy is poured, flatten it with dampened hands to a thickness of ½". Cut the candy into pieces.[31]

CHAPTER 4
Southern Europe

THE ITALIAN TEXANS

1870: 186
1890: 2,107
1900 3,942
1910: 7,190

Joseph is the patron saint of Italy and especially on the island of Sicily. Many old-time Italian Texans still celebrate the Feast of St. Joseph's Altar on March 19 during Lent. Thus, the feast cannot include meat; so instead, the menu includes pizza, spaghetti, vegetables, biscuits, cakes, and pies. A Roman Catholic priest blesses the food the day before the feast. "Back in the old days," on the feast day in Sicily, families would bring into their home the poorest people. Then, according to tradition,

> the master of the house and his family would bathe the feet of the guests, just as Christ did to his disciples before the Last Supper. Then the visitors would be seated at the table. Those served had to take at least a taste of all the food and drink offered, following which the family and invited guests ate. At the end of the feast the leftovers were gathered and distributed to the poor.

When Sicilian immigrants reached Texas during the 1880s, most could speak no English and so felt awkward about choosing poor people who did not understand the language or the custom. Consequently,

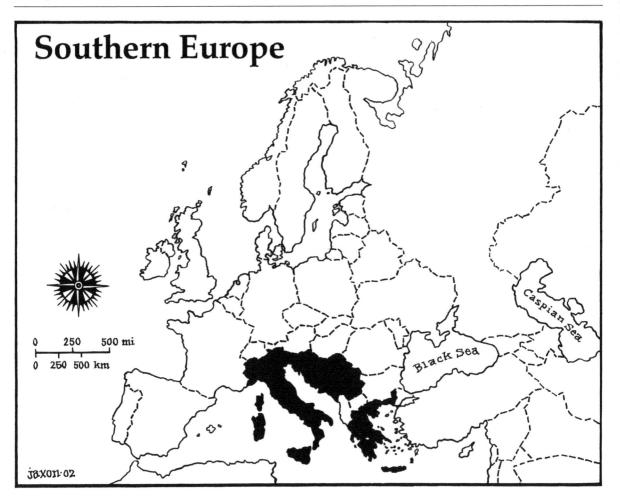

Southern Europe

0   250   500 mi

0   250 500 km

Caspian Sea

Black Sea

J8X011·02

Southern Europe. Map by
Jack Jackson

they selected children of the family, and children of friends, to represent the apostles. The ceremony remained unaltered, with the exception of the foot-washing ritual. Instead, the children would stand on benches or chairs, and those present would kiss their feet as an act of humility. Afterward, the host, his family and friends would carry baskets to the poor in the neighborhood.[1]

Sicilians celebrating St. Joseph's Feast Altar were not the first Italians to come to Texas. One of the earliest Italians was explorer Amerigo Vespucci. As a representative of King Ferdinand of Spain, he wanted to learn if the Americas were different continents or part of Asia. In 1497 he sailed his ship along the Texas coastline. Other early Italians came as soldiers with Spain's Vásquez de Coronado as he explored parts of Texas and the Great Plains during the 1540s. Henri de Tonti represented French interests during 1686 and 1689 when he searched for Sieur de La Salle's ill-fated Texas settlement. However, none of those individuals remained in Texas.

The earliest settlers included a few hardy men such as Vicente Micheli who was a fur trader in Nacogdoches in 1793. He moved to San Antonio in 1806 where he became a rancher and horse trader. Guiseppe Cassini, known in Spanish Texas as José Cassiano, provided food and supplies to Ben Milam's forces when they took San

Food prepared for a celebration of St. Joseph's altar. Institute of Texan Cultures illustration no. 78-64

Antonio from Mexican forces in December of 1835. Another Italian immigrant, Prospero Bernardi, fought at the battle at San Jacinto.

However, it was not until the period of the 1880s and the early part of the twentieth century that most Italians immigrated in larger numbers to Texas, most coming from southern Italy where the people had small farms. With small farms and high taxes, most of the people lived in poverty with bleak futures, so immigration appealed to many. Their numbers swelled in Texas from 186 Italians in the 1870 census to over 7,000 by 1910. In 1980 people who claimed Italian heritage numbered 189,799, and in the 2000 census 4,772 claimed at least one parent from Italy.[2]

The industrious Italians worked at a variety of jobs. Some were railroad workers; others mined coal at Thurber, Texas. Many went

Italian Club band at picnic in Thurber. Institute of Texan Cultures illustration no. 68-2166

into the grocery, bakery, or restaurant businesses, while others engaged in farming, banking, ranching, real estate, wine making, fishing, or boot making.

The oldest licensed winery in Texas claims heritage from the Italian immigrants Frank and Mary Qualia of Milan, in the north of Italy, who came to Del Rio in 1883. They planted grapevines and began a vineyard on their thirty acres using a special kind of goose to eat the insects instead of a pesticide. Within a few years the vineyard produced six thousand gallons of wine. In 2002 the great-grandson of Frank and Mary could still be found plowing the vineyard to produce prizewinning harvests at the family's Val Verde Winery.

Most Italians were Roman Catholic, and the Reverend Bartholomew Rolland arrived in Galveston during 1845 to begin serving the predominantly Italian Catholics there. Adam Janelli introduced the Salvation Army to Texas in 1889, preaching his first sermon in Dallas. He also provided his time and money in support of the publication of *La Tribuna Italiana*. The newspaper, founded in Dallas by Charles Saverio Papa in 1913 and operated by him until its demise in 1962, kept alive for Italian Texans information about their native culture and news from their homeland.[3]

Italians who immigrated to Texas settled not only in the Galveston area but also in Houston, Dallas, Fort Worth, San Antonio, and Austin. Others made their homes in smaller towns such as Dickinson, between Houston and Galveston, as well as along the Brazos River Valley, between Bryan and Hearne, where many bought flood-prone land. The Brazos River Valley Italians had come from Sicily by way of Louisiana where they worked in the sugarcane fields until they earned enough money to buy farms and start the colony in Texas. Though struck by floods in 1899 and 1900, the immigrants remained, forming a large Italian community. By the 1890s Brazos County had one of the largest concentrations of Italian farmers in the United States.

Wherever they settled, the Italians also introduced foods new to the state. Groups such as the Christopher Columbus Italian Society of San Antonio preserved some of their old-world recipes. Founded in 1890, the society served as a benevolent and fraternal association.

Some of their foods seem very "American" today, as their Italian origin is almost forgotten. A true Italian would never buy spaghetti sauce in a jar. Every Italian knows a good spaghetti sauce must simmer on the stove for hours, filling the air with delightful aromas. Italian family meals around large bowls of spaghetti continue to delight the Texans of Italian descent.

Italian Tomato Sauce for Spaghetti

Any meat can be used for a base: chuck roast, a small pork loin, a frying chicken, sausage, or meatballs.

1½ pounds meat
⅓ to ½ cup olive oil
1 large garlic clove, crushed
1 large diced onion
2 8-ounce cans of tomato sauce
6 cups boiling water
salt to taste
1 tablespoon sugar
1 teaspoon sage
1 teaspoon sweet basil
¼ teaspoon fennel
½ teaspoon oregano
1 teaspoon parsley
mushrooms chopped fine

In a skillet, brown the meat in oil and set aside. In the remaining oil, fry the garlic and onion until golden brown. Add tomato sauce and heat thoroughly. Pour into a large pot containing 6 cups of rapidly boiling water. Add salt, sugar, and herbs. Add meat. (If chicken or meatballs are used, do not add until about 30 minutes prior to serving or they will fall apart.) Simmer, uncovered, for 4 to 6 hours, until thick. If thickening occurs too soon, add more boiling water. The secret is to cook it long enough to develop flavor and to cook it uncovered to release the acidity of the tomatoes.

▼▼▼

Italian Meatballs
1 pound lean ground beef
3 or 4 slices of crumbled bread
1 medium egg
1 teaspoon salt
2 tablespoons grated Romano cheese
1 teaspoon chopped parsley
olive oil

Mix all ingredients together, except oil, and shape into tiny balls. Brown the meatballs on all sides in olive oil. Cook slowly until done in the middle and add to the sauce 30 minutes before serving. Serve over spaghetti.

THE GREEK TEXANS

1870: 38
1890: 145
1900: 169
1910: 756

Dallas café owner and Greek immigrant Faithon P. Lucas was once told in the meanest sense that he was a "foreigner." Lucas very politely answered, "I am ashamed that I was not born here, but I came as quickly as I could. And I have done my best to be worthy of America. But I am just as ashamed as your grandfather when he arrived."[4]

Lucas was not the first Greek to make Texas his home. Two of the earliest ones were Pedro and George Serates. They arrived in Texas during 1834 and by 1840 had a dry goods store in San Antonio. A man calling himself "Captain Nicholas" was another early Greek resident. He had been a sailor with the pirate Jean Laffite in 1817. Nicholas so liked Galveston Island that he returned to live there in the 1840s and made his living catching fish and making charcoal.

▼▼▼

Greek Texans Victor Sermas and Michael Colias were chefs in Waco, ca. 1919. Institute of Texan Cultures illustration no. 73-447

However, it was not until the period between 1880 and 1910 that many other Greeks came to Texas. During these years Greece had widespread crop failure, and unemployment was high. Greece also had the mandated military draft, and young Greek men left their country to avoid this required service. An added problem for young Greek men involved marriage. Greece had the dowry system, and a young man who wished to marry had to provide the bride's family with costly goods. Some Greek men could not afford to buy the dowry for a bride.

As a result, young Greek men began to come to America in search of new opportunities. Some of them first found work in Texas as manual laborers, but by saving their money, they prospered enough to start their own businesses such as restaurants, real estate ventures, fishing, grocery stores, and cotton gins. When they had saved enough money, the men often returned to Greece with enough money to pay for a dowry, married, and brought their new wives to Texas. Encouraged by their successes, other Greeks followed them to Texas.

By the early twentieth century, Greeks, although few in number when compared to other European immigrants, had settled in all the major Texas cities: Galveston, Houston, San Antonio, Dallas, Fort Worth, Corpus Christi, Amarillo, San Angelo, Wichita Falls, Waco, El Paso, Austin, and Port Arthur.

Along with settlement came the building of their Eastern Orthodox churches. In Galveston, Greek families joined with Serbian and Russian Texans to establish the Saints Constantine and Helen Eastern Orthodox Church. Its first priest was Greek-born Theoclitos Triantafilides who held services in Greek, Russian, and Serbian.

Other than their regular church services, the Greeks also held special ones, always conducted partly in Greek, as is the custom even today.

Christmas for the Greeks was a solemn occasion preceded by prayer, fasting, or meditation. They observed a strict fast on Christmas Eve. At midnight Holy Communion occurred and they served

Judaism

The people of the Jewish religious faith are present in all countries of the world and represent all nationalities. They are a religious group that bases its beliefs on the Torah, the Prophets, and the Writings, which make up the Hebrew Bible. The Torah consists of the Pentateuch, or the Five Books of Moses, which are also the first five books of the Bible. The Prophets contain the teachings of Isaiah, Amos, and Micah. The Writings have poems, proverbs, psalms, and stories of historical events.

Jews also follow the Mishnah. The Palestinian scholar Rabbi Judah Hanasi compiled the Mishnah from Hebrew oral or spoken laws in about A.D. 200. When additions to it occurred, they appeared in the Gemara. Together, the Mishnah and the

Theoclitos Triantafilides (1833–1916), the first priest of the Serbian, Greek, and Russian Eastern Orthodox Church who came to Galveston in March, 1896. Institute of Texan Cultures illustration no. 68-2724

refreshments immediately afterwards. On Christmas Eve or Christmas Day, children went caroling to Greek homes and stores in exchange for small gifts.

In observance of St. Basil's Day, New Years, a coin is baked in a special cake called a *vasilopita*. When the cake is cut, the finder of the coin is supposed to have good luck in the coming year. . . .

Easter is the most important religious holiday for those of the Greek Orthodox faith. It marks the end of lent and Holy Week is filled with many special services. On Good Friday evening, a flower-covered bier, representing Christ's tomb, is carried in a procession around the church. The Resurrection is commemorated by a Saturday midnight candlelight procession and liturgy, followed by an elaborate breakfast marking the end of the long lenten fast. The food for this breakfast is blessed by the priest and consists of specially prepared breads, cheeses, meats, and pastries. Of particular note is *tsoureki,* a special bread topped with a red Easter egg. Red eggs—symbolizing the blood of Christ—are broken after the service, amid greetings of "Christ is risen," answered by "He is truly risen."

[A Greek] wedding is an hour-long rite, which requires certain stamina, especially on the part of the couple and the best man. The latter stands behind the bride and groom, both of whom wear wreaths. The best man's function is to exchange these wreaths three times during the service. Unconsecrated wine is sipped by the couple as a symbol of the joy they will have. Three times, the couple is led around a temporary altar, placed outside the sanctuary, to the accompaniment of hymns honoring the Virgin, the Apostles, and the Martyrs. A reception follows, at which the bride and groom have the first dance.[5]

Another celebration is Greek Independence Day, which Greek Texans began to celebrate in 1943. In 1821 Archbishop Germanos called for the Greeks to overthrow the Turkish rule of the Ottoman Empire. After an eight-year struggle, Greece finally became an independent country. Greeks in America celebrate that triumph with a church service on the Sunday closest to March 25.

Gemara form the Talmud, which serves as a model for the laws and teachings of Judaism.

Food prepared according to Orthodox Jewish dietary laws is called kosher, which means proper for use. Kosher laws state that meat should never be eaten at the same meal with dairy products. Dairy products must be prepared with separate utensils and served on separate dishes from those which are used for meat. Additionally, Orthodox Jews do not eat pork or shellfish, such as oysters. Kosher slaughtering of animals must be done under the supervision of a rabbi or a ritual slaughterer.

The beliefs of the Jewish people set them apart from their neighbors wherever they lived, and others sometimes responded to these differences with prejudice that caused them to endure discrimination,

▼▼▼

isolation, and often death. Many came to Texas hoping to find a better life where they could live according to their beliefs without enduring the prejudice of others.

Of course, any Greek Texan special occasion involves dancing and foods. The Greek men are especially famous for their rhythmic dances accompanied by bouzouki music. Other dances include their national dance, the *kalamantiano,* and the *tsamiko,* which celebrates a warrior's bravery before going into battle. In the *zembekiko,* one man dances alone followed by another trying to dance better. Two men dance opposite each another when doing the *andekristo.* Probably the best-known dance is the *hasapiko,* or "Zorba's Dance," in which two men dance holding each another's shoulders.[6]

Foods are essential at any Greek Texan festival. Since olive oil and wine were plentiful in Greece, they are used in many of their foods. Along with a dressing, olives, cheese, roast lamb, and wine, some traditional favorite foods for the more than 32,319 (2000)[7] Greek Texans include:

Greek Stuffed Grape Leaves (Dolmathes)
1 16-ounce jar grape leaves
¼ cup chopped fresh mint
2 pounds ground meat

George Pappas, owner of the West Texas Café in San Angelo, Texas, 1930. Institute of Texan Cultures illustration no. 73-642

½ cup rice
salt and pepper to taste
1 tablespoon butter or margarine
2 large onions
2 ½ cups chicken broth or chicken bouillon
¼ cup chopped parsley

The wedding of Angela and Gus Sparto in Ft. Worth, ca. 1914. Institute of Texan Cultures illustration no. 73-461

Scald grape leaves in hot water to remove excess brine. Place meat, salt, pepper, onions, parsley, mint, rice, and ½ cup water or chicken broth in a large bowl and mix well. Pinch stems off leaves and place one by one in a saucer with the shiny side down. Place 1 tablespoon of filling in the center of each leaf at the stem end and carefully fold over top and sides like an envelope to make a roll. Arrange rolls side by side in a large, deep pot. Add butter or margarine together with 2 cups chicken broth and cover. Bring to

▼▼▼

Several Greek Texans in the traditional celebration clothes for Greek Independence Day, March 25, 1934. Institute of Texan Cultures illustration no. 73-911

a boil. Reduce heat and simmer for 30 minutes. Let it cool covered. Reheat to serve, adding lemon-egg sauce at the last minute.

Greek Souflaki (Shish kebab)
3 pounds lamb, pork, or beef
oregano
2 or 3 bay leaves
1 cup olive oil
medium onions, quartered
⅓ cup lemon juice
cherry tomatoes or quartered large ones
bell pepper, cut in 1-inch squares
½ cup wine
salt and pepper
mushroom caps
1 or 2 garlic chopped cloves

Cut meat into 1½" cubes. Combine olive oil, lemon juice, and wine. Pour this marinade over the meat in a large, shallow ovenproof glass pan. Sprinkle with salt and pepper, oregano, and garlic. Add bay leaves and onions. Cover with foil and refrigerate 5 hours or overnight. Remove meat from marinade and stick on wood or metal skewers alternating with tomatoes, onions, peppers, and mushroom caps. Cook skewers over charcoal pit or in broiler. Baste with marinade or melted butter. Cook for 25 or 30 minutes or until cooked to taste. Serve immediately. Makes 9 to 12 servings.

The Callins Brothers' Wigwam Fruit Store in San Antonio, ca. 1930. Institute of Texan Cultures illustration no. 73-904

THE SERBIAN/SLAVIC/CROATIAN TEXANS

1870: 12 est.

1890: 80 est.

1900: 120 est.

1910: no data

The present-day country of Yugoslavia contains people comprising several ethnic groups that include Serbs, Slavs, Croats, and others who were a part of the Austro-Hungarian Empire until 1918. The word Yugoslavia means "land of the South Slavs" and incorporates several countries bordering on the Adriatic Sea. Yugoslavia had not yet been formed when the early immigrants from the area came to Texas.

One of the best known of the nineteenth-century immigrants to Texas was Anthony Francis Lucas. He was born in 1855 and given the birth name Antonio Francisco Luchich or Lucic. He became an engineer and a second lieutenant in the Austrian navy. Austria controlled most of present-day Yugoslavia when Lucas was a young man. A visit to an uncle in Michigan convinced Luchich to stay, and he became an American citizen and changed his name to Lucas. As an engineer, he became interested in underground salt domes and acquired an oil lease on a salt dome called Spindletop near Beaumont, Texas.

Another man, Pattillo Higgins, had drilled at the site but failed to strike oil. Lucas drilled deeper than Higgins and on January 10, 1901, brought in the largest producing oil well then known. Before that, no oil well had produced more than three thousand barrels a day. Lucas's well gushed one hundred thousand barrels a day. At the time, Spindletop made Texas the largest oil producer in the world. As for Lucas, he continued to be a geological consultant until his death in 1921.

Unlike Lucas, the few hundred Croats or Serbs who came to Texas during the late nineteenth century were young men who did not have much formal education. They were laborers and sailors rather

▼▼▼

Cotton jammers at work on a ship in Galveston. Institute of Texan Cultures illustration no. 68-3012

than farmers like most immigrants. Consequently, the Slavs, Serbs, and Croatians looked for jobs in the mines, on the docks, and in the timber industry. The first to arrive in Texas were mostly single men who found work on the docks at the port of Galveston. Called "cotton jammers," they loaded cotton bales onto ships. Some found work cutting timber into railroad ties in the area north of Houston. A few married men saved enough money to bring their wives to join them. Once settled, several of the families became grocers or restaurant owners in Galveston. Some of the more recently arrived immigrants returned home to fight for their homeland in the Balkan Wars and again during World War I.

Croatian Texans, mostly Roman Catholics, became well known not only for their business success but also for their music. One aspect of their music included the *tamburitza,* one of the world's oldest musical instruments. Croatian shepherds invented it about A.D. 500. The first instrument, called a *dangubica,* or "passing of the day," had two strings stretched across a piece of flat wood. Turks, who had conquered the area in the sixth century, gave the instrument the name tamburitza.

Over the years people improved on the tamburitza. They added

St. Edward's University Tamburitza Band in Austin, ca. 1934–37. Institute of Texan Cultures illustration no. 68-3100

two strings to the instrument. Later someone added another two strings. New variations of the tamburitza also appeared. *Bisernitza* is the smallest, whereas the *contrasitza* is a bit larger. The *bisernitza* plays music to accompany a soprano voice, and the *contrasitza* accompanies a contralto voice. There are three *brach* tamburitzas: the *purva brach,* the *droogbrach,* and the *contrabrach.* The first two are the same instrument but play different parts like the first and second violin. The *contrabrach* is the same as a viola in an orchestra. Next in order is the *bugaria,* which resembles the modern guitar. Sometimes, the *bugaria* parts are written so that there may be a first, second, and even a third *bugaria,* but all the instruments are the same. The *berda,* or bass tamburitza, is the largest instrument. It is comparable to the bass viola. In recent years, the *cello brach* has been used like a cello in an orchestra.[8]

Serbian Texans were members of the Serbian Orthodox Church, a branch of the Eastern Orthodox group. The Eastern Orthodox Church came into existence in A.D. 1054 when it split from the Roman Catholic Church. Eastern Orthodox Christians use the original text of the Nicene Creed of A.D. 326, which states that the Holy Spirit comes from the Father, or God. Roman Catholics use a later form of the text, which states that the Holy Spirit comes from the Father and the Son. Instead of a pope, Eastern Orthodox Christians have patriarchs as their church leaders and do not believe anyone is infallible. Priests may marry before their ordination, but only unmarried priests can become Eastern Orthodox patriarchs or bishops. If the wife of a priest dies, he cannot remarry. Eastern Orthodox churches likewise permit members to divorce and remarry but no more than twice. When a divorced church member does remarry, the person must say a prayer for forgiveness at the marriage ceremony.

Once established in Galveston, the Serbian Texans along with Greek Texans and Russian Texans founded the Saints Constantine and Helen Serbian and Eastern Orthodox Greek Church in 1895. Services were conducted in Greek, Serbian, and Russian. Building of the church was mainly due to the efforts and financial backing of Chris Chouke, an early immigrant from the area who had come to Texas in 1855. Chouke worked as a fisherman and dockhand before becoming a well-to-do grocer and rancher on Galveston Island. Although the church building went through the hurricanes of 1900, 1909, and 1915, which damaged the building, determined members of the church rebuilt it after each storm.

Sts. Constantine and Helen Serbian and Greek Orthodox Church in Galveston, ca. 1925–35. Institute of Texan Cultures illustration no. 68-3019

The Serbian Eastern Orthodox churches, as is the case with all Eastern Orthodox churches, continue to follow the Julian rather than the Gregorian calendar in celebrating Christmas, which occurs thirteen days after December 25.

The Serbian Eastern Orthodox Christmas season in Texas begins with greetings of *Hristos se rodi—Vaistnu se Rodi* (Christ is born—Indeed He is born). Christmas Eve is the "Day of the Oak" or *Badnjak,* a time-honored celebration from Yugoslavia. On that day, a specially selected three-year old oak tree is cut by men wearing gloves. They must fell the tree in three strokes with the axe man facing the tree east, blessing himself three times, and throwing a handful of corn in the air. He must repeat: "Good evening, Holy *Badnjak,* happy day to you. I have come to take you home, that you may be our faithful helper in prosperity." The *Badnjak* is cut into three parts, the lowest being the Yule log, which is burned behind the church. This ancient custom began with the pagan festival for the birth of the sun. The upper portion of the tree is decorated and placed in the church. A small tree is also placed in the home.

After vespers on Christmas Eve, the parishioners drink a hot brandy punch and eat bread. Hay is placed on the church floor to remind them of Christ's humble birth and a midnight service is held. Afterwards, the Serbian Orthodox family breaks its fast with cake and a *polazenik* is selected. The *polazenik* is a man whom the family will honor as a special guest on Christmas morning. If anyone else arrives at the home first, the family will not answer the door. When the *polazenik* arrives, he burns a small *badnjak* tree and has breakfast, after which he receives small presents and wishes the family prosperity.

Easter customs among the Serbian Orthodox people begin on Lazarus Saturday, before Palm Sunday. With tiny bells around their necks, the children, singing a hymn, carry willow branches in a procession around the church. Afterwards, a fashion show for the children is held. On Good Friday, the women of the church decorate a table with flowers. The *Plashenitza,* an icon of Christ crucified, is

▼▼▼

placed on the table for a special service at midnight. On Easter morning after service, Easter eggs are broken with greetings of "Christ is Risen—Indeed, he is Risen."[9]

Serbian Texans also have provided Texans with their traditional foods for consumption by all Texans who wish to enjoy them.

Serbian Paprika Chicken
3 to 3½ pounds of chicken pieces
olive oil
salt and pepper
1 large onion, chopped
1 bell pepper, chopped
paprika
6 large tomatoes, skinned or 1 can tomato paste
½ pound fresh mushrooms or 1 can mushrooms
sour cream

Brown chicken in enough olive oil to cover the bottom of a deep skillet. Add salt, pepper, onion, and bell pepper. Sauté. Sprinkle a lot of paprika onto the chicken. Add tomatoes or tomato paste and mushrooms. Cook until chicken is tender. Add dollops of sour cream before serving. Makes 4 to 6 servings.

Conclusion

The nineteenth century is known as the era of the first great migration to America, and the people are often referred to as the "old" immigrants. People came from virtually all the countries of Europe, though most came from northern and western Europe. Europe in the 1800s was undergoing great change as the start of the industrial revolution displaced many skilled craftsmen. The feudal systems of Europe were crumbling, and peasant farmers often in debt lost their lands from crop failures or disease.

Land was the big motivator for virtually all immigrants whether they came alone, in a family unit, or with a group based on a common religion, a common geographic region in Europe, or kinship ties. Land in most European countries was simply not available for purchase. Most families were large with everyone's labor needed, but with medical and nutritional advances, there was a sharp decline in the death rate of children, causing overpopulation in some countries. In wealthier countries, inheritance laws caused some sons to leave and seek their fortune abroad since only the oldest son inherited the family estate. There was little chance that the other sons could find or afford land to begin a home for their own families—land was just too scarce, too costly, and too highly taxed. So they came to the western frontier of America—to Texas—where land was in abundance and lots of hard work provided an opportunity to build a home of their own.

Others came to escape religious persecution and prejudice. Jewish immigrants came from many European countries. Jews were outsiders in Christian Europe, and state policies often prohibited them from owning farms and working in certain jobs, thus forcing them to live in separate communities. So Jews from Germany,

Poland, Russia, and numerous other countries joined in the great European migration.

Some men came for adventure such as the early explorers, the unrealistic Frenchmen at La Réunion colony, and the English lords with their polo ponies and top hats.

Even when the future looked bleak, many Europeans found it difficult to make the decision to leave their homeland, move thousands of miles to some unknown place, and live among strangers with a different language. Once they made the decision to leave, there was the formal paperwork that was needed to immigrate, plus all the decisions about what to pack for a place where few knew the climate or what type of living arrangements they would have to make. Finally, the prospective immigrants had to sell or give to other family members property and all their remaining personal goods. At last they purchased tickets and boarded the ship, but once aboard they found it was often overcrowded, smelled bad, and the food had bugs in it. People got sick and some died, but finally Texas appeared on the horizon. And after all the trauma those aboard had endured, many of the European immigrants were not welcomed to Texas. They were strange and different.

Some groups experienced prejudice and discrimination. Something made them different: language, dress, religion, customs, or owning better land than their neighbors. The neighbors most likely were only one or two generations away from Europe themselves, but still the new arrivals were often rejected.

Many settlers came because they had heard about Texas from a family member or a fellow countryman writing home. Often the glowing reports were misleading. However, Jacob Raphael de Cordova, born in Jamaica of Jewish descent, who became known as the "Land Merchant of Texas," had a more realistic view of the situation. De Cordova published the first official map and encyclopedia of Texas; his enthusiasm for Texas was unlimited. His 1858 book, *Texas: Her Resources and Her Public Men,* encouraged people to move to Texas. In it, De Cordova offered the following practical advice to future immigrants:

Jacob Raphael de Cordova (1795–1870), a Texas land merchant. Institute of Texan Cultures illustration no. 68-2491

Beware those who paint Texas as an earthly paradise. I have no idea of giving a false coloring to our state. It is not a paradise, but it is a country where the poor man can easily obtain land. And when he has it, he can always raise enough to support his family.

Do not be fooled into thinking that you are coming to a country where there is everlasting spring or summer. Our winters are cold enough to require warm clothing, blankets, and comforters. And while packing these, do not forget to include a small library.

Select a body of land yourself, after thoroughly examining it, so it will suit your own needs. . . . For a man of small means, 160 acres will be quite enough. Where a man has the actual capital to invest, without crippling his farming operation, he may purchase 320 or 640 acres. But rarely is it advisable to take over 1280 acres.

Much of this land can be purchased for from $1.50 to $2.50 per acre, although choice acres are sold as high as from $5 to $8 or more per acre. . . .

To mechanics who thoroughly understand their business and are in those trades that a new country requires, we say come on. You will do well.

As regards merchants and clerks, there are openings left for those who are ready and willing to devote their time and attention to business. But of this group, our country cannot bear too large a supply.

To teachers, both male and female, who are competent to teach, there are many openings. . . . Texas as yet does not require many professors. What she wants is a body of intelligent teachers who are able and willing to teach the basics of a plain English education to the new generation.

To politicians I say, stay where you are. We have no room for you.

De Cordova's advice was useful for a growing state, but virtually all groups experienced difficulties once they arrived—if they survived the long, difficult ocean voyage. Depending on their location in Texas, they had to contend with harsh weather conditions such as droughts, floods, or hurricanes. There were serious diseases, often fatal, such as cholera, yellow fever, and malaria. Whatever resources the families had brought with them, it still took years of old-fashioned hard work to reap the comfortable life of their hopes and dreams. Some did not prosper, and some returned to their native land.

▼▼▼

A second massive wave of southern and eastern European immigrants arrived at the beginning of the twentieth century, but Texas had changed. All the good land had been claimed, and the remaining acreage was expensive. The Alien Land Law of 1892 affected many who had dreamed of their own homes and acreage. Though some immigrant farmers got sufficient money to buy land working as sharecroppers and tenant farmers, many experienced hard times as the industrial revolution got under way. With the frontiers of Texas gone, the agrarian economy changed, and the new immigrants came to the towns and cities where they found work as laborers in factories and stores and faced different obstacles than those who had come before. As they learned the language, they merged into the general population, retaining little of their ethnic heritage. They became Texan.

The history of Europe has been about war and battles begun by national leaders anxious to expand their tax base and enlarge their empires. Many men left to avoid serving in the military, but this came to a screeching halt by 1914. With the advent of World War I, European nations were reluctant to allow the departure of men needed for military service. Additionally, with submarine warfare and military vessels on the high seas, oceanic travel became more risky. So immigration stalled until after the war when new conditions once again encouraged growth in immigration to Texas.

Today, many Texans are doing family genealogies. They may be fifth and sixth generation Texans—many of European descent. In the process, they will trace their lineage back to Europe and learn that the old trunk in the barn really did come with their great-great-grandparents or that the sauerkraut they have on New Year's Day is a tradition left over from their distant European heritage. For many of today's Texans this may be all that remains of the once vibrant cultural legacies of their ancestors. Many foods and recipes that came "from the old country" are now just considered part of American cuisine. The rural ethnic communities of the nineteenth century have almost disappeared with little but their names to remind us of their cultural past.

Nevertheless, the stream of people coming to Texas over the decades has influenced the character of its people. Noted for a willingness to take risks and try new ventures as well as for independence and optimism, this country of immigrants from around the world continues to be strong and visionary. The values and beliefs of the early European settlers to Texas continue to provide the foundation for many of our laws, educational institutions, forms of entertainment, and religious affiliations as well as the food on our tables. The cultural diversity of Texas is a proud and cherished legacy that is continuously enriched by the new immigrants who remind us of our privileges and unique status in the world.

Notes

INTRODUCTION

1. Irving L. Gordon, *American History,* 2d ed. (New York: Amsco School Publications, 1996), p. 359.
2. Jesse A. Ziegler, *Wave of the Gulf* (San Antonio: Naylor Company, 1938), p. 202.
3. Thomas W. Cutrer, *The English Texans,* p. 122.

CHAPTER 1. WESTERN EUROPE

1. *The French Texans,* p. 18.
2. Jo Lyday, "Jambalaya," in *The Folklore of Texan Cultures,* ed. Francis Edward Abernethy, p. 49.
3. "French," *The New Handbook of Texas Online* (hereinafter referred to as *HOTO*), http://www.tsha.utexas.edu/handbook/online/index.new.html (Dec. 5, 2002).
4. Philip Graham, ed., "Texas Memories of Amelia Barr," *Southwestern Historical Quarterly* (Apr., 1966): 473–98, quote on p. 487.
5. John L. Davis, *Texans One and All,* p. 11.
6. John L. Davis and Philip L. Fry, "English," *HOTO,* http://www.tsha.utexas.edu/handbook/online/index.new.html (Dec. 5, 2002).
7. Zoe Alexander, "The Last Warrior Piper," undated, The John MacGregor Memorial Service, the Alamo (San Antonio, Mar. 6, 1993), presented to Daughters of the Republic of Texas by Clan Gregor Society, American South West Chapter.
8. "5th Annual Scottish Highland Games of Houston, Texas, May 4, 1975," in "Scottish" Vertical Files (San Antonio: Institute of Texan Cultures).
9. John L. Davis, "Scots," *HOTO,* http://www.tsha.utexas.edu/handbook/online/index.new.html (Dec. 4, 2002).
10. Adapted from a tale told by Mike Welch, in *Straight Texas,* ed. J. Frank Dobie (Austin: Texas Folklore Society, 1937).
11. Graham Davis, *Land! Irish Pioneers in Mexican and Revolutionary Texas* (College Station: Texas A&M University Press, 2002), pp. 6, 239.
12. John Brendon Flannery, *The Irish Texans,* pp. 47–51.
13. Ibid.

14. Phillip L. Fry, "Irish," *HOTO,* http://www.tsha.utexas.edu/handbook/online/index.new.html (Dec. 4, 2002).

15. Adapted from Robert J. Duncan, "Footprints of Wooden Shoes," in *The Folklore of Texan Cultures,* ed. Abernathy, p. 184.

16. Ibid.

17. Ibid.

18. 2000 Texas census figures online, http://factfinder.census.gov/bf/_lang=en_vt_name=DEC_2000_SF3_U_DP2_geo_id=04000US48.html (June 24, 2003).

19. Adapted from Samuel P. Nesmith, *The Belgian Texans,* pp. 5–6.

20. Ibid.

21. Adapted from William T. Field, Jr., *The Swiss Texans,* p. 9.

22. Ibid.

23. "Costumes" in "Switzerland Texans" Vertical File (San Antonio: Institute of Texan Cultures).

24. William Field, "Swiss," *HOTO,* http://www.tsha.utexas.edu/handbook/online/index.new.html (Dec. 5, 2002).

CHAPTER 2. NORTHERN EUROPE

1. John L. Davis, *The Danish Texans,* p. 62.

2. Adapted from Davis, *Texans One and All,* p. 19.

3. Adapted from Davis, *The Danish Texans,* p. 53.

4. Adapted from Davis, *The Danish Texans,* pp. 120–21.

5. Adapted from Susan Lucas and Sara Clark, eds., "Community Celebrations in Danevang" in *The Folklore of Texan Cultures,* ed. Abernethy, pp. 194–96.

6. C. A. Clausen, ed., *The Lady with the Pen: Elise Waerenskjold in Texas,* pp. 35–37.

7. Ibid., p. 59.

8. *The Norwegian Texans,* p. 10.

9. Palmer H. Olsen, "Frank Bean," in *The Folklore of Texan Cultures,* ed. Abernethy, p. 252.

10. Adapted from Sadie J. Hoel, "The Norse of Bosque County," in *The Folklore of Texan Cultures,* ed. Abernethy, pp. 246–49.

11. W. Phil Hewitt, "Norwegians," *HOTO,* http://www.tsha.utexas.edu/handbook/online/index.new.html (Dec. 9, 2002).

12. Seaholm, "Genealogy of the Seaholm Family."

13. Larry E. Scott, *The Swedish Texans,* p. 186.

14. John Peter Sjolander, *Salt of the Earth and Sea* (Dallas: P. L. Turner Company, 1928), p. 96.

15. Scott, *The Swedish Texans,* pp. 35–37.

16. Art Leatherwood, "Swedes," *HOTO,* http://www.tsha.utexas.edu/handbook/online/index.new.html (Dec. 9, 2002).

CHAPTER 3. EASTERN EUROPE

1. Terry G. Jordan, "Germans," *HOTO*, http://www.tsha.utexas.edu/handbook/online/index.new.html (Dec. 9, 2002).
2. Glen L. Lich, *The German Texans*, pp. 57–59.
3. Caroline Von Hinueber, "Life of German Pioneers in Early Texas," p. 2.
4. Frederick Law Olmsted, *A Journey through Texas*, pp. 177–79.
5. Lich, *The German Texans*, p. 182.
6. Ibid., p. 162.
7. Adapted from Julia Estill, "Customs among the German Descendants of Gillespie County (in 1928)," in *The Folklore of Texan Cultures*, ed. Abernethy, pp. 146–47.
8. German tale collected by Carolyn Mankin in *Singers and Storytellers*, ed. Mody C. Boatright, Wilson M. Hudson, and Allen Maxwell.
9. From collection of E. R. Bogusch, Gilbert Jordan, and Curt Schmidt, in Lich, *The German Texans*, p. 177.
10. Adapted from Estill, "Customs among the German Descendants," pp. 149–50.
11. Sylvia Ann Grider, *The Wendish Texans*, pp. 30–32.
12. Ibid.
13. Ibid., pp. 63, 65.
14. Ibid., p. 75.
15. *The Melting Pot: Ethnic Cuisine in Texas*, p. 222.
16. T. Lindsay Baker, *The Polish Texans*, p. 28.
17. Ibid., p. 31.
18. Ibid., pp. 88, 91.
19. Adapted from Ann Carpenter, "O Ty Polshi!" in *The Folklore of Texan Cultures*, ed. Abernethy, pp. 212–13.
20. Jan L. Perkowski and Jan Maria Wozniak, "Poles," *HOTO*, http://www.tsha.utexas.edu/handbook/online/index.new.html (Dec. 9, 2002).
21. Annie Hanicak Foyt, and Olga Foyt Slimp, interview by Marguerite Louise Hanicak, transcript in possession of the author.
22. W. Phil Hewitt, *The Czech Texans*, pp. 6–7.
23. Adapted from W. Phil Hewitt, *Land and Community: European Migration to Rural Texas in the 19th Century* (Boston: American Press, 1981), p. 41.
24. Ibid., pp. 15–16.
25. Ibid., pp. 20–21.
26. Olga Pazdral, *Czech Folklore in Texas*, pp. 125–26.
27. Clinton Machann, "Czechs," *HOTO*, http://www.tsha.utexas.edu/handbook/online/index.new.html (Dec. 9, 2002).
28. James Patrick McGuire, *The Hungarian Texans* (San Antonio: Institute of Texan Cultures, 1993), p. 186.
29. Adapted from *Alice Daily Echo*, Jan. 28, 1951.

▼▼▼

30. 2000 Texas census figures online, http://factfinder.census.gov/bf/ _lang=en_vt_name=DEC_2000_SF3_U_DP2_geo_id=04000US48.html (June 24, 2003).

31. Recipe of Mary Anne Nagy, St. Nicholas Day Celebration, Dec. 8, 1980, Texas Catholic Conference of Ethnic Community Affairs, Our Lady of the Lake University, in "Hungarian Texan" Vertical Files (San Antonio: Institute of Texan Cultures).

CHAPTER 4. SOUTHERN EUROPE

1. W. Phil Hewitt, *The Italian Texans,* p. 15.

2. Valentine J. Belfiglio, "Italians," *HOTO,* http://www.tsha.utexas.edu/ handbook/online/index.new.html (Dec. 4, 2002).

3. Hewitt, *The Italian Texans,* p 15.

4. *The Greek Texans* (San Antonio: Institute of Texan Cultures, 1974), p. 11.

5. Adapted from *The Greek Texans,* pp. 30–31.

6. Ibid.

7. 2000 Texas census figures online, http://factfinder.census.gov/bf/ _lang=en_vt_name=DEC_2000_SF3_U_DP2_geo_id=04000US48.html (June 24, 2003).

8. Adapted from a St. Edward's University, Austin, Texas, publication in "Yugoslav Texans," Vertical Files (San Antonio: Institute of Texan Cultures).

9. Ibid.

Bibliography

Abernethy, Francis Edward, ed. *The Folklore of Texan Cultures.* Austin: Encino Press, 1974.

Baker, T. Lindsay. *The First Polish Americans: Silesian Settlements in Texas.* College Station: Texas A&M University Press, 1979.

———. *The Polish Texans.* San Antonio: Institute of Texan Cultures, 1982.

Boatright, Mody C., Wilson M. Hudson, and Allen Maxwell, eds. *Singers and Storytellers.* Dallas: Southern Methodist University Press, 1961.

———. *Texas Folk and Folklore.* Dallas: Southern Methodist University Press, 1954.

Clausen, C. A., ed. *The Lady with the Pen: Elise Waerenskjold in Texas.* Northfield, Minn.: Norwegian-American Historical Association, 1961.

Cutrer, Thomas W. *The English Texans.* San Antonio: Institute of Texan Cultures, 1985.

Davis, John L. *The Danish Texans.* San Antonio: Institute of Texan Cultures, 1983.

———. *Texans One and All.* San Antonio: Institute of Texan Cultures, 1998.

Dobie, J. Frank, ed. *Straight Texas.* Austin: Texas Folklore Society, 1937.

Field, William T., Jr. *The Swiss Texans.* San Antonio: Institute of Texan Cultures, 1981.

Flannery, John Brendon. *The Irish Texans.* San Antonio: Institute of Texan Cultures, 1995.

The French Texans. San Antonio: Institute of Texan Cultures, 1993.

Gallup, Sean N. *Journeys into Czech-Moravian Texas.* College Station: Texan A&M University Press, 1998.

The Greek Texans. San Antonio: Institute of Texan Cultures, 1974.

Grider, Sylvia Ann. *The Wendish Texans.* San Antonio: Institute of Texan Cultures, 1982.

Hewitt, W. Phil. *The Czech Texans.* San Antonio: Institute of Texan Cultures, 1998.

———. *The Italian Texans.* San Antonio: Institute of Texan Cultures, 1994.

The Jewish Texans. San Antonio: Institute of Texan Cultures, 1974.

Kownslar, Allan O. *The Texans: Their Land and History.* New York: McGraw-Hill and American Heritage, 1972.

Lich, Glen L. *The Federal Republic of Germany and Texas.* Bonn, Germany: Inter Nationes, 1986.

———. *The German Texans.* San Antonio: Institute of Texan Cultures, 1996.

Linck, Ernestine Sewell, and Joyce Gibson Roach. *Eats: A Folk History of Texas Foods.* Ft. Worth: Texas Christian University Press, 1989.

Lorenzen, Lilly. *Of Swedish Ways.* Minneapolis: Dillon Press, 1971.

Machann, Clinton, and James Mendl. *Krasna Amerika: A Story of the Texas Czechs, 1851–1939.* Austin: Eakin Press, 1983.

McGuire, James Patrick. *The German Texans.* San Antonio: Institute of Texan Cultures, 1970.

———. *The Hungarian Texans.* San Antonio: Institute of Texan Cultures, 1993.

The Melting Pot: Ethnic Cuisine in Texas. San Antonio: Institute of Texan Cultures, 1997.

Nesmith, Samuel P. *The Belgian Texans.* San Antonio: Institute of Texan Cultures, 1975.

The Norwegian Texans. San Antonio: Institute of Texan Cultures, 1985.

Olmsted, Frederick Law. *A Journey through Texas*. New York: Dix, Edwards, and Company, 1857.

Ornish, Natalie. *Pioneer Jewish Texans: Their Impact on Texas and American History for Four Hundred Years, 1590–1990*. Dallas: Texas Heritage Press, 1989.

Pazdral, Olga. *Czech Folklore in Texas*. Austin: University of Texas Press, 1942.

Scott, Larry E. *The Swedish Texans*. San Antonio: Institute of Texan Cultures, 1990.

Seaholm, Ernest Mae. "Genealogy of the Seaholm Family." Eagle Lake, Texas, August, 2001. In possession of the author.

Skrabanek, Robert L. *We're Czechs*. College Station: Texas A&M University Press, 1988.

Vertical Files, Austrians, Belgians, Czechs, Danes, Dutch, English, French, Germans, Greeks, Hungarians, Irish, Italians, Jews, Norwegians, Poles, Scots, Swedes, Swiss, Wends, and Yugoslavs. San Antonio: Institute of Texan Cultures.

Von Hinueber, Caroline. "Life of German Pioneers in Early Texas." *Quarterly of the Texas State Historical Association* (January, 1899).

Winegarten, Ruthe, and Cathy Schechter. *Deep in the Heart: The Lives and Legends of Texas Jews*. Austin: Eakin Press, 1990.

Index

▼▼▼

▼▼▼

ISBN 1-58544-352-2